Overview

Everyone encounters a wide range of difficulties, mishaps, and obstacles. You can think of a "problem" as anything from a mild irritation – like a sticky keyboard – to a complete disaster that puts your job or even your life at risk.

A problem is a question or situation that causes doubt or perplexity, or presents a difficulty. It's something that needs to be corrected or overcome so you can achieve a desired state. A problem often requires a unique or creative solution.

In other words, you have a "problem" when you have a goal but can't readily see how to reach it – when you have to think, plan, and devise suitable actions to solve the problem and achieve the goal.

Barriers to achieving your goals can vary widely in kind and importance. Your problem might be as small as spilling coffee on your tie right before going into an important business meeting.

Or it could be much more serious – say if the laptop your presentation was on got stolen and you didn't have a backup.

But if you know just what to do in response to a problem, it's no longer a real problem. This is because there's no doubt or complexity involved for you – the path of action you need to take to achieve your goal is clear.

Problems come in two basic varieties. The first is an unexpected disruption to the normal course of things. For example, your supplier fails to deliver crucial items or your car breaks down on your way to a conference. You may or may not know what caused the disruption.

The second type is a gap between your current state and a desired state, or goal. If you aren't sure how to bridge that gap, you have a problem.

For example, you might want to find ways to meet a new consumer need. Or you might want to improve your own efficiency in terms of managing your time, meeting sales targets, or designing products.

Everyone needs to solve problems, from the trivial to the life-threatening, at some point. This course covers the following:

- a tried-and-tested problem-solving model you can adapt to suit any problem,
- how to recognize and prevent the mind traps and procedural pitfalls people often fall into, and the
- different skills and competencies needed to solve a variety of problems.

*

64. Problem-Solving and Decision-Making Strategies

Consider a game of chess. At almost any point in the game, several alternative moves are possible. Depending on your strategy, each of these may be equally effective. Similarly, there's typically more than one way to approach any problem you encounter.

In a game of chess, your chances of winning depend on how well you assess the board after each player's move, on identifying all your options and choosing the best ones, and on executing your strategy properly.

Like in chess, your ability to solve problems effectively depends in part on your using a sound problem- solving model.

It also depends on the skills you bring to the table – including your analytical, creative, and practical skills.

People differ in the ways they typically approach problems. For example, one person may tend to focus on systematically evaluating hard facts. Another may prefer to visualize a problem and use more creative methods to generate solutions. Sometimes a particular approach is called for – but in other cases, no one approach is right or wrong.

Each way of approaching a problem has both advantages and disadvantages. Recognizing these, and identifying your dominant approach, is a good first step for improving your problem-solving abilities.

Identifying your dominant problem-solving style can make you aware of the blind spots, or weaknesses, in your style. As a problem solver, you'll want to avoid blind spots that affect your ability to solve problems effectively.

Once you know where your strengths and weaknesses lie, the next step is to work on improving your problem-solving skills. You can develop your analytical, creative, and practical skills, both to address your weaknesses and to refine your strengths.

Analytical skills

Analytical skills will help you to consider and solve problems that require logic and systematic reasoning.

Creative skills

Creative problem-solving skills enable you to come up with original and unconventional ideas for solving problems.

Practical skills

Practical problem-solving skills will permit you to solve day-to-day problems in the most pragmatic way, using your experience and willingness to adapt.

A final important consideration for solving

problems effectively is learning how to prevent bias from affecting your results.

People's mental processes and their underlying motives and emotional needs can prevent them from perceiving problems – and possible solutions – objectively. These human factors introduce bias into problem-solving.

So to solve problems effectively, it's important to recognize and counter bias when it arises. In this course, you'll learn how to improve your ability to solve problems in several ways:

- by identifying the dominant problem-solving style you have and determining your strengths and weaknesses,
- by recognizing the different types of skills associated with effective problem solving and learning about strategies for developing these skills, and
- by recognizing and overcoming the different types of bias that can creep into and compromise the problem-solving process.

Ultimately, analyzing your problem-solving style, skills, and biases can help you identify your weaknesses so that you can devise a program to develop them into strengths.

**

Suppose your laptop stops launching the

software you've legally installed, and you bring it in for repairs. Are you happy when the technician just tells you to reinstall all software? Shouldn't the technician spend time investigating the problem to ensure that the reinstallation resolves the problem and prevents it from reoccurring? Just as your technician needs to dig deeper to find the true cause of your laptop's malfunction, in business you need to dig deeper to find solutions to business problems.

Business solutions can't be dependent on one person's intuition. Many different factors that may not be apparent at first – but remain hidden below the surface – may play a role in why the photocopier is causing delays.

Neither should one stakeholder's opinion dictate one solution. So just because your team members tell

you that a second color photocopier will reduce the waiting times, other, more cost-effective, and long- term solutions may exist if you investigate further.

To discover the underlying factors of a problem, or the root cause, you need to study and analyze the problem objectively and honestly. In other words, you need to dig deeper using fact-based analysis.

It's easy to address a symptom of a problem and then think that you've problem solved effectively. In

64. Problem-Solving and Decision-Making Strategies

the photocopier example, delayed printing is the symptom. Buying a second one may be the obvious solution because two photocopiers double the output. But is this the most effective solution? Aren't you merely addressing a symptom? Usually, the symptom and the cause are two different things, and you need to base your solution on the cause, not the symptom.

Buying a second photocopier is an effective solution, only if it addresses the root cause of the problem.

It isn't an effective solution if you discover that the root cause was initially hidden from you. For example, you discover a colleague is using the color photocopier to make prints for a business she runs on the side. Buying a second copier will only make her believe she can double her private output.

Or you discover that your team members are moved to the end of the print roster whenever another team requires prints. If this is the root cause, then buying a second photocopier is unlikely to reduce delays in the long run and possibly add tension between those involved.

In this course, you'll learn that digging deeper helps you solve problems effectively.

You'll learn about the different types of fact-based analysis tools used to objectively determine the root causes of a problem.

And, once you've determined the cause, you'll learn how to identify potential solutions and how to choose the most appropriate one.

***

Research suggests that you make up to 50,000 decisions every day. Many of these decisions are relatively unimportant – like what color tie to wear to work or what kind of sandwich to have for lunch. Others are more critical. For example, business decisions to target a new market or to fire an unproductive worker – or personal decisions such as how you react in an emergency – can have significant consequences.

In spite of this, most people aren't trained to make sound decisions. Instead they often try to cope by imitating what others have done in similar situations, or by falling back on what worked in the past – although past approaches may not be valid in new situations.

To help you make effective decisions, you can follow a systematic decision-making process. First you need to establish a context for success. Next you frame the issue properly. Then you generate and evaluate a number of alternatives. And finally, you choose the best alternative.

1. Establish a context for success

64. Problem-Solving and Decision-Making Strategies

To make successful decisions, you first need to create an environment – or context – that's conducive to decision making. This includes carefully considering who's involved and where it takes place.

2. Frame the issue properly

When you frame an issue, you need to have a clear understanding of the situation and know what the real issue is. After all, you can't make a decision, if you don't understand the situation.

3. Generate alternatives

You need to generate as many possible alternatives as you can. You can't make a decision unless you have alternatives to choose from.

4. Evaluate the alternatives

Some solutions may not be possible in certain situations, so it's important to evaluate each alternative in context.

5. Choose the best alternative

Once you've evaluated the alternatives, you can decide which one is best for your situation.

As well as following a clear process, you should be aware of the decision-making style you use. Each style is useful in certain situations. There are four main types of decision-making styles:

- the authority or expert style, in which you act as the boss or expert and make decisions

without considering the opinions of others,
- the consultative style, in which you gather input from others but retain the responsibility for final decisions,
- the majority or voting style, in which the most popular decision is chosen – even if a minority of people disagree with it, and
- the consensus style, in which you search for a solution that everyone agrees with and can support.

Effective decision making isn't an easy skill to learn, but it has many benefits, including increased productivity and stronger workplace relations. This course will equip you with the skills you'll need to achieve these goals.

In this course, you'll learn about these decision-making fundamentals:
- the basics of effective decision making, including a five-step decision-making model your team can use,
- different decision-making styles that you can adapt to suit a range of situations, and
- the factors that affect which decision-making style you should use in a particular situation.

****

Like most people, you've probably made decisions in the past that, in hindsight, you wish had

64. Problem-Solving and Decision-Making Strategies

been different. Often it's crucial to make the right decisions before you commit limited resources of time and money to implementing them. But it's not always possible to foresee all the consequences of a decision or to decide on the direction that's best.

Using a range of decision-making tools can simplify the process of reaching decisions and help you identify the best alternatives, rationally and systematically.

Decision-making tools can help you generate alternatives you may not otherwise have considered. This ensures decisions are based on an awareness of all the possible options.

The tools can also help you to evaluate the alternatives rationally by assessing their relative strengths and shortcomings. They can make it easier to judge whether an alternative offers real benefits.

Ultimately you arrive at a decision by choosing one of the available alternatives. Decision-making tools can guide you through this process. They enable you to manage the process of making intelligent, appropriate decisions.

Many tools and techniques are available to decision makers. Some commonly used tools you may find helpful include: the nominal group technique, abbreviated to NGT; Return on Investment, commonly known as ROI; the devil's advocate technique; plus-minus-interesting – or PMI – analysis; and the ease-and-effect matrix.

Nominal group technique

The nominal group technique is useful in generating alternatives and selecting preferred alternatives. It helps to prevent the usual drawbacks of group-based decision making – such as groupthink, majority influence, and polarization – by keeping suggestions and evaluations anonymous.

ROI

You calculate ROI to compare the financial implications of decision alternatives. This helps you to place numeric or financial values on qualitative costs and benefits and therefore select alternatives based on how they'll affect your bottom line.

Devil's advocate technique

The devil's advocate technique helps you to view an alternative from a range of perspectives. It provides a structure for critical debate and analysis of an alternative's weak points and associated assumptions.

PMI analysis

PMI analysis enables you to weigh the pros and cons of an alternative, and to consider the consequences of choosing to implement it.

The ease-and-effect matrix

An ease-and-effect matrix enables you to

64. Problem-Solving and Decision-Making Strategies compare decision alternatives based on how easy they are to implement and on how effective they're likely to be in meeting goals. It's a useful tool for comparing large numbers of alternatives.

In this course, you'll learn how to apply the common decision-making tools and techniques. Each decision you make, however, is called for by a particular context and brings its own set of challenges. So you need to determine for yourself what tools to use in each situation. The more tools you have at your disposal, the better the decisions you can make.

*****

You make decisions every day of your life. What should you wear to the office today? Which project should you fund? By when do you need to have approval for your proposal? How much can you spend on a venue? Sometimes making a decision is simple; but at other times, it can be tough.

Consider the case of Loretta. She likes her job and gets along really well with her colleagues. However, she's just been offered a new, more challenging job with a higher salary. Taking the job will mean spending longer hours away from her family. However, it also means her family will finally be able to afford to buy a house.

Like in Loretta's case, you can identify a tough

decision if one or more of these factors applies: you have to deal with unknowns and conditions of uncertainty

- you need to make compromises – or trade-offs – because no one alternative perfectly satisfies all your objectives, and
- you need to balance logic and intuition as part of the decision-making process.

Deal with uncertainties

When dealing with uncertainty, decisions can become "messy." Whatever you decide, a certain amount of ambiguity remains because you can never know all the variables that play a role in the decision you make.

Loretta's dealing with a lot of uncertainties. For example, the new job offers her more money, but how much overtime will she be expected to work per week? Will it be possible for her to take work home with her so she won't spend much more time at her new office than she's spending at her current job?

Make trade-offs

You often need to balance the pros and cons of every possible alternative before you can make a decision. The final decision is likely to be a trade-off because you'll have to give up something, no matter what you decide. However, you can ensure

64. Problem-Solving and Decision-Making Strategies

you choose the one with the least amount of negative consequences for you.

Both taking the job and not taking it have pros and cons. Whatever compromise Loretta makes, she can make a decision that complements some, if not all, her aspirations for a more challenging and higher-paid job, and her wish to fulfill her responsibilities to her family.

Balance logic and intuition

Following your logic – or making a decision based purely on facts – may not always result in your making the best decision, especially when a decision is complex, ambiguous, or urgent. You should listen to your intuition as well.

Your intuitions spring from your inherent knowledge, including your experiences, memories, and conditioning. They shouldn't be dismissed. But the trick in effective decision making is to balance both logic and intuition.

Loretta's gut feeling, for example, is to take the new job. To make the best decision, she should balance this intuition with a logical evaluation of the pros and cons.

******

To help ensure you choose the best alternative when you're faced with a tough decision, you should follow these steps:

- gather relevant information and informed opinions from your colleagues and other stakeholders,
- limit the amount of information you evaluate to what you really need to make a sound decision, so that you don't get overwhelmed by irrelevant details,
- focus on the most important elements and goals of the decision so that you don't get sidetracked, and
- account for both subjective and objective factors when evaluating your alternatives, to merge logic and intuition.

In this course, you'll learn how to tackle the three areas of difficult decision making. You'll learn how best to handle uncertainty in decision making. You'll also learn how to identify the best possible alternative when it's necessary to make trade-offs. And you'll learn how to balance intuition and logic to make the most effective decisions.

Using these strategies won't shield you from difficult decisions in business or in your personal life. However, they'll make tough decisions simpler and assist you in making better decisions.

Problem Solving: The Fundamentals

The Problem-solving Model
Problem-solving Mind Traps
Dealing with Problem-solving Traps
Problem-solving Skills and Competencies

The Problem-solving Model

To solve problems effectively, you need to use a good problem-solving model.

The six-step model is a tried-and-tested approach. Its steps include defining a problem, analyzing the problem, identifying possible solutions, choosing the best solution, planning your course of action, and finally implementing the solution while monitoring its effectiveness.

Solving a problem

Natalie has a problem. She's often exhausted and is battling to meet her deadlines. She keeps trying to focus on solving the problem, but it seems like the more determined she is to fix it, the more she struggles to find a solution.

Like most people, Natalie sees problem solving as a single action – you have a problem, you fix it. But to find long-term, viable solutions, even for problems that seem simple, you need to take a step back and approach the process systematically.

Problem solving is the mental process you follow when you have a goal but can't immediately see how to achieve it. It's a process that depends on you – how you perceive a problem, what you know about it, and the end-state you want to reach.

Solving a problem involves a number of cognitive activities:

- ascertaining what the problem really is,
- identifying the true causes of your problem and the opportunities for reaching your goal,
- generating creative solutions to the problem,
- evaluating and choosing the best solution, and
- implementing the best solution, then monitoring your actions and their results to

ensure the problem is solved successfully.

Clearly, problem solving is not a one-step process. Your success will depend on whether you approach and implement each of the stages effectively. The best way to do this is to use a well-established, systematic problem-solving model.

The six steps of problem solving

Problems vary widely, and so do their solutions. Sometimes a problem and its solution are clear, but you don't know how to get from point A to point B. At other times, you may find it hard to define what's wrong or how to fix it.

Regardless of what a problem is, you can use a six-step problem-solving model to address it. This model is highly flexible and can be adapted to suit various types of problems. It also comes with a flexible set of tools to use at each step.

The model is designed to be followed one step at a time, but you may find that some stages don't require as much attention as others. This will depend on your unique situation.

Question

Think of something that's bothering you at the moment.

What do you think is the first step you should take to solve your problem?

Options:
1. Define the problem
2. Think of the best way to solve the problem
3. Call in the experts

Answer

Option 1: This is a great start. Although the

situation might seem clear-cut, you may just be looking at a symptom of the real problem.

Option 2: Although this step is clearly a necessary one, it comes much later in the problem-solving process than you might think. First you need to define your problem before you can find a way to solve it – what's really the issue?

Option 3: If someone's available to help with a problem, that's wonderful. However, you still need a good problem-solving approach to follow, whether you're alone or part of a team. And even if experts are available to help, it's likely they need your input – starting with a clear definition of what the problem is.

The first thing to do is to define the problem. This crucial step involves digging deeper to identify what it is that needs to be solved. The more clearly a problem is defined, the easier you'll find it to complete subsequent steps.

A symptom is a phenomenon or circumstance that results from a deeper, underlying condition. It's common to mistake symptoms for problems themselves – and so to waste a lot of time and effort on tackling consequences of problems instead of their causes.

To define a problem, you can use a tool such as

64. Problem-Solving and Decision-Making Strategies

gap analysis. This involves comparing your current state to the future state you want to be in, to identify the gaps between them. For example, Natalie knows that she is currently over-tired and missing deadlines, and that she wants to feel better-rested and meet her deadlines. The space between her current and desired states is the gap she needs to bridge by solving her problem.

The next step is to analyze the problem. You decide what type of problem it is – whether there's a clear barrier or circumstance you need to overcome, or whether you need to determine how to reach a goal. You then dig to the root causes of the problem, and detail the nature of the gap between where you are and where you want to be. This will help you see past the distracting symptoms to the real issues that underlie them.

The five-why analysis is a tool that will help you get to the heart of the problem. Ask "Why?" a number of times to dig through each layer of symptoms and so to arrive at the problem's root cause.

For Natalie, the five-why analysis begins with the question "I keep missing my deadlines. Why?" She answers this honestly "Because I always run out of time." Then she subjects this answer to a second "Why?" which reveals that she's not managing her time properly. Subsequent "Whys" will lead her closer to the real root cause of the problem, and thus the best solution.

You can get to the root of a more complicated problem using a cause-and-effect diagram. A cause is something that produces an effect, result, or consequence – or what contributed to the current state of affairs. Categories of causes include people, time, and the environment. In Natalie's case, a cause-and-effect diagram reveals that her crowded, noisy office environment, the interruptions from people, and unreasonable deadlines are the main factors contributing to her problem of missing deadlines.

Next identify as many potential solutions as you can – in other words, try to think of ways to close the gap. Brainstorm creatively – ask lots of questions about the who, what, where, when, and how of the causes to point to various possibilities. Don't limit yourself by considering practicalities at this stage; simply record your ideas.

Once you've generated as many ideas as you can, you need to evaluate them so you can choose the best solution. In evaluating your ideas, more options could present themselves.

You could do this by rating each possible solution you came up with in step 3 according to

64. Problem-Solving and Decision-Making Strategies

criteria such as how effective it will be, how much time or effort it will take, its cost, and how likely it is to satisfy stakeholders. What these criteria are will depend on the problem at hand.

Once you've decided what the best solution is, you need to map out your plan of action in this way:

- determine what steps must be taken, designating tasks where necessary,
- decide on deadlines for completing the actions and estimate the costs of implementing them, and
- create a contingency plan in case of unforeseen circumstances so that if anything goes wrong with your plan, there's a "plan B" in place.

Typically, this stage involves narrowing down the possible ways to implement the solution you've chosen, based on any constraints that apply.

For instance, you have identified training employees in a particular skill as the solution to a problem. During planning, you determine that the available budget only allows for e-learning and remote training, so these are the types of training you'd plan to provide.

You should draw up an action plan that includes the who, what, and when of your proposed solution. The complexity of the plan will depend on the situation, but it should include these basic elements.

As the final step, you need to implement the solution. This is an ongoing process. You need to ensure the required resources remain available and monitor progress in solving the problem; otherwise, all the work you've done might be for nothing. You can use a checklist to track what has been done, and note what still needs to happen.

Question

Matthew works for a small photocopying business. He's been asked to figure out why the business spends so much money on fixing or replacing damaged equipment, and to take steps to improve the situation.

Sequence the six steps of the problem-solving process he should follow.

Options:

A. Use a checklist to monitor the implementation

B. Complete an ease and effect matrix to see which option would be best

C. Brainstorm to generate ideas for solving the problem

D. Do a gap analysis to help pinpoint the problem

E. Draw a cause-and-effect diagram to list the

64. Problem-Solving and Decision-Making Strategies

possible reasons for the problem

F. Draw up an action plan to figure out what everyone should do

Answer

Do a gap analysis to help pinpoint the problem is ranked the first step.

As the first step, Matthew needs to define what the problem really is. At the moment, the machines are breaking down more frequently than they should be. He'd like to end up with a situation in which the machines require only routine maintenance.

Draw a cause-and-effect diagram to list the possible reasons for the problem is ranked the second step.

Once Matthew is sure he knows what the problem is, the second step is to analyze the problem to determine its root cause or causes. The wear and tear on the machines is only a symptom – perhaps they're of inferior quality, or maybe they aren't serviced often enough to prevent breakdowns.

Brainstorm to generate ideas for solving the problem is ranked the third step.

As the third step, once the real cause of the problem is clear, Matthew needs to brainstorm creatively in order to identify as many solutions as possible. By thinking outside the box, he might find a solution he wouldn't have thought of otherwise.

Complete an ease and effect matrix to see which option would be best is ranked the fourth step.

After coming up with as many possible solutions as he can, Matthew will need to choose the best of these. An analysis of the proposed solutions can help him narrow down the options based on their likely benefits, and on the effort and resources they'll take to implement.

Draw up an action plan to figure out what everyone should do is ranked the fifth step.

As the fifth step, once he's chosen a solution, Matthew needs to plan how best to implement it. This will depend on any constraints. For example, hiring a full-time technician may not be feasible, but existing staff members could undergo maintenance training.

Use a checklist to monitor the implementation is ranked the sixth step.

As the final step, Matthew needs to implement his chosen solution and review the implementation on an ongoing basis to ensure that it's working. If not, he'll have to make adjustments or even fall back on a contingency plan.

So there are six things you need to do to solve a problem effectively. First you define the problem clearly and analyze it to determine root causes. Then

64. Problem-Solving and Decision-Making Strategies

you identify potential solutions and choose the best solution from those you've generated. You plan the course of action you'll take and, finally, implement the solution and review the progress that's made in solving the problem.

Remember that this model is highly adaptable. Although you shouldn't skip any of the six steps, you can tailor the amount of time you spend on each stage based on the demands of your unique situation.

For example, Frank, a freelance writer, needs someone to illustrate his children's book. His problem is clear – he needs a new artist. So it won't take him long to define or analyze the problem.

But it will take a while to think of ways to locate candidates and to choose someone whose drawing style will match his work. So these steps – identifying solutions, choosing the best option, and planning action – will take longer.

Question

The six-step problem-solving model can benefit you in a number of ways.

How do you think it can help you solve a problem more effectively?

Options:

1. It makes it unnecessary to involve a large

number of people when making a decision, thereby saving time and money

2. It ensures that when you select a solution, you're guided by a firm understanding of the causes of the problem

3. It ensures that you evaluate the success of a solution and make corrections if necessary

4. It makes solving a problem a conscious, objective, and fact-driven task

5. It enables you to jump straight to solutions, without wasting any time

6. It ensures you generate as much information and insight about a problem as possible

Answer

Option 1: This option is incorrect. Actually, it's often useful to get input from as many people as possible when you're solving a problem. Different people might have unique insights about what the problem really is, and could contribute potential solutions.

Option 2: This option is correct. By defining and analyzing a problem to get to its root cause or causes, you'll avoid wasting time and resources in addressing only the symptoms of the problem. Instead, you'll be able to focus on finding a real, long-term solution.

Option 3: This option is correct. By reviewing

64. Problem-Solving and Decision-Making Strategies

progress as a chosen solution is implemented, you'll be able to ensure that the problem really is being solved – and to make adjustments where necessary.

Option 4: This option is correct. Using the six-step problem-solving model enables you to uncover the best solution to a problem, systematically and objectively. There are a number of methodical tools that can simplify each step and make it more objective.

Option 5: This option is incorrect. If you try to solve a problem with the first thing that springs to mind, you might miss out on more effective solutions. Or worse, you might misinterpret the problem or fail to recognize its real cause.

Option 6: This option is correct. The model encourages you to dig deeper, analyze, and be creative. With all the information you gather by following the steps it includes, you'll find solutions easier to pinpoint and implement.

The six-step problem-solving model, and the tools it provides, is an effective, systematic approach to problem solving. By following each step consciously, you can ensure that generating solutions is a fact- driven, objective, and reliable process.

It encourages you to dig deeper to the root cause,

allows you to get input from others, to be creative when finding solutions, and to monitor your solutions to make sure they're working. So by following this model you're more likely to come up with good, original, lasting solutions.

Problem-solving Mind Traps

Problem solving can be hampered by a variety of mind traps, which include holding on to initial ideas; defending prior choices; selecting supporting information in a way that supports bias; making assumptions; and succumbing to conformity.

Each step in the problem-solving model is more vulnerable to certain mind traps than to others, but all traps impair your ability to solve problems objectively and systematically.

Barriers to problem solving

Early in the twentieth century, many experts believed that radio waves could not be transmitted over long distances – for example, over an ocean. They believed that because the Earth is a sphere, and radio waves travel in a straight line, the waves would travel out into space rather than to the intended target.

However, inventors like Guglielmo Marconi and Nikola Tesla refused to be constrained by the thinking of their peers. Their revolutionary work in the field of radio transmission proved the experts' assumptions wrong, and laid the foundations for much of the advanced communication technology being used today.

Throughout history, problem solvers in all fields have struggled to break through barriers that constrained their thinking. In fact, it's part of human nature to have mental baggage, and often it's only by getting past this that real solutions to problems can be found.

So some barriers to effective problem solving arise from the way people think. At other times though, it's the process followed to address a problem that has flaws. So there are two main types of barriers to problem solving. You can think of

64. Problem-Solving and Decision-Making Strategies
these as mind traps and process traps.

Mind traps
Mind traps are internal. They reside in the mind of the problem solver.

Process traps
Process traps are external. They are problems or mistakes in the approach used to solve a problem.

Jim is renovating his house. Two months into the work, he worries that the renovations are going to look disastrous. There's still time to alter the plans, but Jim decides to stick with the existing plans – trusting to the initial vision he had, instead of what he sees now. He ends up ruining the look of large sections of his house.

In this case, Jim's inadequate response to the problem led to disaster. His response came about because he fell into a mind trap.

Mind traps can prevent you from understanding what the real problem is, pinpointing its causes, or "thinking outside the box" to come up with helpful solutions.

Types of mind traps

Common mind traps that prevent effective problem solving include being influenced by people's initial ideas, defending prior choices, selecting supporting information based on bias people already have, making assumptions, and conformity.

A popular saying states that "first impressions last." When considering a problem, the same can be said of first thoughts – the initial ideas you have when first considering the problem.

The starting point of your thinking – whether an idea, a particular fact, an estimate, or something else – usually influences your subsequent thinking about the problem.

Say you make a decision to invest a small sum in the stock market. You discuss this with a friend, who says "Perhaps you could try one of those startup technology companies – or no, maybe just do your research carefully and see what the trends are."

You go about collecting information about your options. However, the initial idea of choosing a startup technology company is hard to shake.

It colors your thinking as you assess the possibilities, and eventually it's the option you

64. Problem-Solving and Decision-Making Strategies

choose. But if your friend hadn't mentioned the idea in passing, it's likely your choice would have been different.

The initial ideas trap is most likely to affect the second and fourth steps of the problem-solving model – when you analyze a problem and when you choose what appears to be the best solution. Initial ideas about the nature of the problem and the best way to address it can color your thinking at these steps and prevent you from engaging in honest, thorough analysis of problems and solutions.

It's important to avoid this mind trap because the roots of a problem are often deep; and if the problem and solutions are not analyzed properly, you could end up with less effective solutions.

Do you remember Jim, who ruined his house by continuing renovations when he saw that it was going to be a disaster? Jim's mistake is a classic example of defending prior choices.

When you're faced with a problem, it can be tempting to make a decision that protects your previous decisions. This is particularly true if your prior choices involved costs to you or your company. If you've already invested in a decision, it's hard to change it – even if doing so would be much less costly in the long run.

This mind trap has a particularly strong impact

on the fourth step of the problem-solving model – when you choose what seems the best alternative from possible solutions.

Now say you need to choose and then purchase a new delivery vehicle for your company. You immediately favor a particular truck model. To find out the pros and cons of the model, you then contact the manufacturer who produces it – effectively ensuring that what you're told will confirm your original bias in favor of the model.

Even when people try to be neutral, mentally they've often decided on an alternative before they even begin investigating. As a result, it's common to seek out supporting information that confirms an initial bias.

The trap of selecting supporting information based on an initial bias is especially likely to affect the second, fourth, and sixth steps of the problem-solving model.

2. Analyze the problem

Your analysis of a problem will depend on the information you use. But your initial bias about which alternative solution is best can influence your decisions about where to collect information and about which information is significant. This becomes a cycle – because you're selective in

64. Problem-Solving and Decision-Making Strategies

choosing data, it in turn appears to confirm your original bias.

4. Choose the best solution

Because initial bias skewed the evidence on which you based your problem analysis, your interpretation of the solution will also be skewed. Also, you may be more likely to choose an alternative you originally favored than to seriously consider other alternatives.

6. Implement solution and review progress

You're likely to be more lenient in judging the success of a solution if it's one you originally favored. You'll eagerly seek evidence that it's working, and may discount evidence that it's not.

Consider another scenario. A clothing store is struggling to compete with a new store in the area. The embattled store owner assumes that this is because the competitor stocks more popular clothes. She tries to solve the problem by bringing some new clothing ranges into stock. Unfortunately, this solution fails and the store continues its downward spiral.

But the real problem was not the popularity of the clothing. It was the price. The rival store offered lower prices, and its bargains attracted more and more customers.

In this case, the store owner's ingrained assumptions simplified her view of the problem, causing her to overlook hard evidence and other potential solutions.

Even if an assumption appears reasonable or based on common sense, by nature it's a belief that hasn't been verified. Especially when assumptions are strongly held, they can lead problem solvers to overlook or even ignore the facts.

The first four steps in the problem-solving model are particularly vulnerable to the mind trap of assumptions.

1. Define the problem

The store owner assumed that the problem lay in the merchandise she was selling. So she failed to identify the real problem, which was competition over price.

2. Analyze the problem

Based on her assumption about the nature of the problem, the store owner analyzed the types of clothing sold in each store. She determined the average age of customers in the area and investigated trends indicating growing demand for high-fashion items – including fashionable sportswear – among less youthful sectors of the market.

64. Problem-Solving and Decision-Making Strategies

3. Identify potential solutions

The store owner generated potential solutions for the wrong problem. She considered options for altering her buying decisions, for example to stock more fashionable clothing ranges and introduce new lines – such as sportswear – into her store.

4. Choose the best solution

Because the list of potential solutions was focused purely on type of clothing – and not price – the store owner's choice of solution operated on a false assumption. As a result, the solution ultimately failed.

By nature, human beings are social creatures. Whether people like it or not, the actions of others often influence them. This leads to another type of mind trap – that of conformity.

Conformity, or "groupthink," can lead problem solvers to accept the consensus of a group instead of being critical in assessing a problem and its possible solutions.

A sales manager needs to improve communications among his team members. He asks them for ideas, and they all quickly agree that the convenience of an online forum would suit them well. Though he doubts that members will use it consistently, he sets up a forum. Sure enough, communication on the forum drops off over time. Instead of conforming with the wishes of the group, the manager should have evaluated the forum solution carefully and explored other solutions as well.

The conformity trap can impact every step of the problem-solving model, but is likely to affect the fourth and sixth steps most.

In a group, everyone else's support for a particular solution may convince you – or even pressure you – to support it too.

And when it comes time to evaluate the success of the solution, the group may have a vested interest in reaching a positive conclusion.

Question

Match each mind trap to its corresponding example.

Options:

A. Initial ideas
B. Defending prior choices
C. Selecting supporting information
D. Assumptions
E. Conformity

Targets:

1. Susan keeps coming back to the first design that she liked, though subsequent designs had some

64. Problem-Solving and Decision-Making Strategies

better features

2. Youssef travels to a show during a dangerous storm to avoid wasting money he'd spent on tickets

3. Ruth wants to buy a certain laptop model so she asks a friend who has one to tell her about its best features

4. Josie avoids asking colleagues for input because she's sure they're too busy

5. Michel's hesitations about the proposed process wane when he sees how popular it is

Answer

The trap of initial ideas anchors problem solvers in their preliminary impressions and can prevent them from giving due consideration to other ideas.

Protecting prior choices, even when it's better to discard them and move on with a revised plan, may cause problem solvers to make unwise decisions.

By asking the friend to tell her only about the laptop's good features, Ruth is selectively seeking information that supports her desire to buy one.

The assumption that her colleagues won't be part of the solution will likely prevent Josie from considering useful solutions that require input from others.

When the majority or group opinion influences your perception of an issue, the mind trap of conformity is in effect.

Sorin Dumitrascu

The mind traps that commonly compromise the problem-solving model are consequences of the way people naturally think and behave. However, you can overcome these barriers by being aware of them, and by selecting and using the appropriate process tools.

Question

Match each mind trap to the statement that best describes how it's likely to affect the problem-solving model.

Options:

A. Trap of initial ideas
B. Trap of defending prior choices
C. Trap of selecting supporting information
D. Trap of assumptions
E. Trap of conformity

Targets:

1. Prevents the team from probing for the real problem or evaluating every proposed solution

2. Prejudices in the selection of solutions

3. Compromises the data used to judge the problem, solutions, and outcome

4. Prevents you from objectively defining a problem, digging for root causes, generating solutions, and choosing the best one

64. Problem-Solving and Decision-Making Strategies

5. Pressures teams into choosing a popular solution and judging the implementation a success

Answer

Initial ideas are difficult to let go of, but they can prevent problem solvers from objectively evaluating either the problem or the alternative solutions.

The tendency to defend prior choices most often affects the step in which the best solution to a problem is chosen. After having invested in one decision, it becomes difficult to change it – even if a new decision is called for.

Selecting supporting information based on an initial bias is likely to compromise the steps in which you analyze a problem, choose the best solution, and then implement the solution and review progress.

Assumptions about a problem and its possible solutions can compromise the first four steps: defining a problem, analyzing it, identifying potential solutions, and choosing the best solution.

Conformity affects every step of the problem-solving model but is most likely to compromise the steps of choosing the best solution step and implementing and evaluating the solution.

Dealing with Problem-solving Traps

Problem solving can be hampered by a variety of both mind traps and process traps. Common process traps include failing to involve the right people, taking on problems that are too vague, bypassing analysis, and failing to plan solution implementation and evaluation.

You can overcome process traps by using a systematic problem-solving model. You can also use specific strategies to overcome each of the common mind traps.

Countering mind traps

Mind traps can seriously derail the problem-solving process, but fortunately, there are a variety of strategies you can use to counteract their effects.

To counteract the trap of initial ideas, you should explore different sources and perspectives.

By broadening your horizons, you're more likely to find the real roots of a problem and to generate a wider range of possible solutions.

You should follow this guideline whenever you problem solve, but it's especially important during the earliest steps of the problem-solving model.

To minimize the trap of defending prior choices, you follow these guidelines:
- give your goals priority – focus on achieving a particular goal rather than becoming attached to a particular decision or process,
- get a neutral opinion – consult someone who does not have a vested interest in your prior decisions, and
- accept your mistakes, remembering that everybody makes mistakes sometimes and that it's better to move on than to hold onto past decisions.

Question

You've already formed a preference for a particular solution to a problem.

What do you think are ways to avoid the mind trap of selecting information that supports your initial bias?

Options:

1. Ask open questions
2. Ensure you gather information about the option you favor
3. If possible, discuss the solution you favor with someone who has already implemented the same solution to a similar problem
4. Actively seek out information that contradicts your initial view

Answer

It's important to ask open questions rather than leading ones, and to make an active effort to seek out information that contradicts your initial views. These are good ways to avoid bias in the way you gather information about a problem and its possible solutions.

Option 1: This option is correct. Asking yourself and others open questions such as "What do you think of this idea?" is a good way to get opinions that balance out your initial bias.

Option 2: This option is incorrect. If you focus on gathering information only about the option you

64. Problem-Solving and Decision-Making Strategies

already favor, the results will give you a selective vision only of this option.

Option 3: This option is incorrect. Someone who's already chosen a particular alternative isn't likely to contradict your choice of the same alternative, so you're likely just to gather support for your own initial bias.

Option 4: This option is correct. Seeking out information that contradicts your initial view will help you overcome bias in the data you gather.

To avoid selecting supporting information, you should ask yourself and others open questions such as "What are your thoughts on this solution?" – rather than asking leading questions such as "Why should I be keen about this solution?" Another good strategy is to examine counterarguments and information that conflicts with your own views.

One way to fight the trap of assumptions is to identify what your assumptions are and check their validity. Take the position of an outsider and ask basic questions to challenge your assumptions, like "Why do I think this way?" or "Why do we do things like this?"

Another strategy is to focus on data. Investigate hard data, rather than relying on mental simplifications or falling victim to personal bias.

You can also change the way you view the problem – restate the problem in new terms or break it down into its simplest components.

To protect yourself from the trap of conformity, shield yourself from social influence and persuasion.

Remember that the popular opinion is not always correct. You should also be willing to defend well-founded viewpoints, even if they are unpopular.

Question

Match each mind trap to the guidelines for avoiding it.

Options:

A. Initial ideas
B. Defending prior choices
C. Selecting supporting information
D. Assumptions
E. Conformity

Targets:

1. Explore different sources and perspectives
2. Give your goals priority, get a neutral opinion, and accept your mistakes
3. Ask open questions and examine counterarguments
4. Check the validity of preconceived notions, focus on data, and change the way you view a

64. Problem-Solving and Decision-Making Strategies problem

5. Shield yourself from social influence and persuasion, and be willing to defend well-founded viewpoints

Answer

Accessing a wider range of information makes it more likely you'll find the real roots of a problem, and generate a wider range of possible solutions, without being overly influenced by initial ideas.

Prioritizing your goals, getting objective opinions from others, and accepting your mistakes can help you let go of prior decisions and move on constructively.

Asking open questions and examining counterarguments can help you overcome bias in the way you select relevant information about a problem and its possible solutions.

Checking the validity of your assumptions, focusing on objective data, and experimenting with new perspectives on a problem can all help you avoid relying on assumptions.

Shielding yourself from influence and being willing to defend well-founded viewpoints will protect you from conforming with the consensus view, in cases where this view isn't the best or most accurate.

Problem-solving process traps

Mind traps aren't the only pitfalls to watch out for in problem solving. Process traps, which are flaws or errors in the way the problem-solving model is approached, can also prevent you from finding effective solutions.

Four main types of process traps are common:
- failing to involve the right people in addressing a given problem,
- taking on problems that are too large, vague, or general,
- bypassing proper analysis of a problem, and
- failing to plan the implementation of a chosen solution or evaluation of its success.

Failing to involve the right people

Failing to involve the right people – those who know a problem best and are affected by it directly – is a common mistake. It can result in you choosing a solution based on insufficient information that isn't viable or suitable.

For example, IT experts develop a highly sophisticated program to improve the efficiency of a company's accounting processes. If they do this without consulting staff in the Accounting Department, the program may fail to address the company's actual needs – or prove to be too complex for the staff to use.

Taking on problems that are too vague

It can be frustrating and demotivating to take on a problem that's too big, vaguely defined, or general. This type of process trap can cause confusion and loss of momentum.

Say you're tasked with "improving productivity" in a large multinational company. Unless you focus on more specific goals – like improving the productivity of particular processes or departments – each of the steps of the problem-solving model is likely to be overwhelming.

Bypassing analysis

Problem solvers often bypass the analysis stage if they're under pressure to produce solutions. This can result in superficial causes being blamed, or weak and faulty solutions being accepted.

Say a critical system is malfunctioning. Someone under pressure may immediately opt to replace the full system – rather than isolating and replacing a single faulty component.

Failing to plan or evaluate the implementation

Sometimes, just coming to a solution is so exhausting that problem solvers give up when it comes to planning how to implement the solution and evaluate its performance. This can prevent a potentially viable solution from succeeding.

For example, to help ease administrative backlog, a property agency decides to give its sales agents new, customized notebook computers. However, the customization plans take so long that, by the end of planning, no one has considered the most cost-effective way to distribute the notebooks. The notebooks are handed out only to a few agents, and down the line, no one bothers to check if the administrative backlog has dropped significantly.

You can avoid common process traps by ensuring you use a systematic and well-defined problem- solving model. In the six-step model, each of the steps prevents particular types of process traps.

Failing to involve the right people

You address the trap of failing to involve the right people when you first define and analyze a problem, and assemble a problem-solving team.

Assembling a team is not an "official" part of the six-step model, but it is vital for ensuring you get the most relevant information you can about a problem and its possible solutions.

Taking on problems that are too vague

64. Problem-Solving and Decision-Making Strategies

The step of defining a problem clearly can prevent you from attempting to address problems that are too large or vague. By defining a problem well, you make it discrete – and ensure it can be subjected to further, useful analysis.

Bypassing analysis

In the six-step model, the steps of analyzing a problem, identifying possible solutions, and choosing the best solution ensure that you don't misdiagnose a problem, or simply accept the first feasible idea for addressing it. They encourage you to dig deeper, assess possible causes and solutions, and be critical.

Failing to plan or evaluate the implementation

The steps of planning action and implementing the solution and reviewing progress ensure that you don't fail to plan how to put a solution into action, to evaluate its success, and to have a backup plan in case it isn't working.

Question

A bank customer service agent has tackled a problem, but with unsatisfactory results.

Which process traps has the agent fallen into?

Options:

1. Failing to plan action or evaluate the

implementation
   2. Taking on a problem that's too vague
   3. Bypassing analysis
   4. Failing to involve the right people

Answer

Option 1: This is a correct option. Because the agent was in a hurry, he didn't provide the customer with a contact person for the weekend, in case the customer required further assistance. The agent therefore had no way to check the effectiveness of his solution.

Option 2: This is an incorrect option. The problem was clearly defined because the customer specified what information she needed.

Option 3: This option is correct. Because the agent was under pressure to resolve the call, he didn't analyze the customer's real needs. As a result, he provided a report that was not the most effective solution for the customer's problem.

Option 4: This option is incorrect. The agent had access to the required information and had the expertise to deal with the query. In this case, it wasn't necessary for him to involve others in addressing the problem.

Recognizing and addressing traps

Perhaps the most dangerous trap of all is one that lurks behind all the other traps – that of complacency. If you're complacent, you'll fail to be vigilant to the traps, and it's unlikely you'll identify problems clearly or arrive at the best possible solutions.

To counter complacency, it's essential that you remain alert and aware of how various mind and process traps can compromise your effectiveness in solving problems.

It's also critical that you be honest about your own weaknesses and encourage others to alert you to these when necessary.

Case Study: Question 1 of 2
Scenario

Jenny is a customer service agent at a large supermarket. She runs into a problem when a customer – who does not have a receipt – needs his heater replaced or repaired. She tries to solve the problem, but falls into several traps.

Test your ability to recognize and counteract problem-solving traps by answering the questions in the
given order.

Question

What effects have mind traps and process traps had on the problem-solving process?

Options:

1. Jenny didn't have a backup plan, in case her chosen solution failed
2. Jenny's desire to defend a prior choice prevented her from seeing the real problem
3. Jenny's initial definition of the problem was tainted by selective supporting information
4. The trap of conformity had an impact on Jenny's choice of solutions
5. Jenny let an assumption taint her evaluation of potential solutions

Answer

Option 1: This is a correct option. Because Jenny failed to plan implementation of her chosen solution, she didn't consider what to do if her solution failed.

Option 2: This option is incorrect. Jenny's analysis cut through the symptoms to reveal what the real problem was: the customer didn't have proof of purchase.

Option 3: This is an incorrect option. Jenny used selective supporting information in the analysis stage and the solution selection stage – not in the definition stage.

64. Problem-Solving and Decision-Making Strategies

Option 4: This option is correct. John's favorable opinion to Jenny's initial sympathy for the customer influenced her thinking throughout the process.

Option 5: This is a correct option. Jenny assumed her manager would sympathize with the customer, and this influenced her choice of solution.

Case Study: Question 2 of 2

What actions should Jenny take to avoid these traps in future?

Options:

1. Seek advice from more colleagues, and go with the majority opinion
2. Focus on facts and customer data, and try to perceive the problem from a new perspective
3. Ensure she plans the implementation of her solution, including a contingency plan
4. Ask leading questions that support her own viewpoint

Answer

Option 1: This option is incorrect. Jenny shouldn't base her decisions on conformity to popular opinion, because the correct decision is based on merit – rather than social acceptance. Instead, she should shield herself from social influence.

Option 2: This is a correct option. Considering

historical data and alternate views will help Jenny transcend her assumptions and personal bias.

Option 3: This option is correct. Proper planning will allow Jenny to put her solution to maximum effect, evaluate its success or failure, and shift to a backup plan if needed.

Option 4: This is an incorrect option. Asking leading questions is likely to result in biased information, which will impair the effectiveness of the problem-solving process.

Problem-solving Skills and Competencies

There are three kinds of problem-solving skills: analytical, practical, and creative. Each type is most effective for solving certain types of problems. Some complex problems require a combination of the skill types.

A competency is a set of factors needed for success. Important problem-solving competencies include drive and initiative, using a methodical approach, teamwork, astute problem analysis, and innovative thinking.

Problem-solving skills

Amrit, Steven, and Tom work for a company that is experiencing some communication problems. Sometimes different employees work on the same task simultaneously while at other times tasks aren't done at all. They've been asked to solve the problem.

They make a great team because each of them has a unique way of approaching and solving problems. Follow along as they describe their approaches to problem solving.

Amrit: *At business college, we were taught to approach things rationally and logically. So I gathered as much information as I could about the communication system and the chain of command to isolate where the fault lies.*

Steven: *I've been working for similar companies for over a decade, so I know all the ins and outs of management politics. I didn't have to think about it too hard – there's obviously a problem with the way managers delegate tasks.*

Tom: *I'm new here, but I'm sure we can improve the system in a number of ways. I've got lots of ideas I'd like to try out.*

64. Problem-Solving and Decision-Making Strategies

Each team member has a unique approach to problem solving. Amrit has a more theoretical approach that she applies systematically.

Steven has valuable hands-on experience and in-depth knowledge of the company.

And Tom thinks outside the box to find new ways of doing things.

Psychologist Robert Sternberg identified three types of intelligence, which all people use at some time or another. Analytical intelligence involves the use of logic and reason to maneuver from A to B. Practical intelligence involves finding the best fit between your actions and the demands of the situation, often by applying skills learned through experience. And creative intelligence involves thinking "outside the box" to come up with novel ideas. Solving different problems will require different types of intelligence.

You typically use an analytical approach when a problem is abstract, requires you to analyze information to find a solution, and is logical in nature, or when a familiar situation or an expected course of events is disrupted, and you need to identify the obstacles, address them, and get back on track.

If two of your employees are having an argument, it might be best to use an analytical approach to solve the problem. You gather information from each person to get an accurate picture of the situation and then isolate a solution that satisfies both parties.

Question

Based on their description earlier in the topic, which member of the team – Steven, Amrit, or Tom – is likely to display analytical intelligence?

Options:

1. Steven
2. Amrit
3. Tom

Answer

Option 1: This option is incorrect. Steven displays practical intelligence that comes from his many years of experience.

Option 2: This is the correct option. Amrit is a rational, logical person who likes to apply her mind to problems. She displays analytical intelligence.

Option 3: This is an incorrect option. Tom displays creative intelligence. He thinks outside the box to find fresh solutions.

Practical skills are used to solve problems in everyday life, typically involving material things. They aren't easy to learn or control, because they

64. Problem-Solving and Decision-Making Strategies draw on the problem solvers' extensive knowledge and experience solving similar problems. The problem solver will most likely find a solution intuitively.

"Street-wise" people and those who have lived a long, rich life often demonstrate practical intelligence. For example, a senior manager who smoothes over any conflict and knows intuitively how to deal with different people, demonstrates practical intelligence. The manager can do this because of the variety of people she has met over the years.

Practical problem solving doesn't involve a high degree of critical thinking, but it does rely on your ability to set your emotional reactions aside and accept the way things are. If your computer deletes your work for the day, reacting emotionally isn't going to get the information back. It's more practical to move on and find ways to make up for lost time.

Practical skills can't be acquired or sharpened as readily as creative or analytical skills can, so organizations can't encourage people to formally acquire this kind of intelligence. But they should recognize, encourage, and reward the application of practical problem-solving skills.

Problems involving unforeseen complications typically require analytical or practical problem-solving skills to break down the problem and overcome it. But unusual or unfamiliar problems that don't come with a lot of information often require lateral, creative thinking – in other words, creative intelligence.

When you know where you want to be in the future, but don't know how to get there, a creative solution may be just what you need.

To design a new product that meets a consumer need none of your competitors have addressed, for example, you need fresh ideas. Developing improvement goals also typically requires creative thought. It helps to think outside the box to discover ways to improve your sales targets, lower your budget, or improve employee morale.

Creative problem solving starts with being open to the idea that new, fresh solutions are possible. You put aside your assumptions and suspend judgment of your ideas while you come up with them.

One method is to ask yourself lots of questions to free your mind from your usual thinking patterns and kick-start your imagination. You might ask "What would be an unusual way of doing this?" or even "What would a child suggest?" Asking "What if...?" as many times as possible can help you escape your own preconceptions.

64. Problem-Solving and Decision-Making Strategies

Some problems require a combination of the different problem-solving approaches. If you stay open to the possibility of using a variety of skills, you'll have an advantage over people who tend to fall back on the same way of meeting challenges.

Question

Harry's printer has stopped working. Although he has never really thought about how printers operate, he needs to fix the problem so he can print an important document.

Which activity demonstrates the type of skill best suited to solve the problem?

Options:

1. Harry steps back from his initial anxiety, and draws on his experience of broken televisions to think of a solution

2. Harry tries to get an accurate picture of the situation by systematically ruling out possible problems with the printer

3. Harry frees his mind of assumptions about how printers work and thinks laterally to find as many fresh solutions as he can

4. Harry keeps trying to print the document in case the printer sorts itself out

Answer

Option 1: This is an incorrect option. This

intuitive, practical approach isn't suitable for this problem because of Harry's lack of experience with fixing printers.

Option 2: This is the correct option. The best approach in this example is for Harry to assume there must be a way of making the printer work and to set out to find it – using logical, analytical thinking to solve the problem.

Option 3: This is an incorrect option. This creative approach isn't appropriate for a technical problem like this one. A logical appraisal of the situation would be the best way to isolate the cause.

Option 4: This is an incorrect option. Ignoring the problem won't make it go away. Harry should tackle the problem head-on by using logic and reason to figure out a solution.

Problem-solving competencies

A skill is an ability to use your knowledge to accomplish a task. Skills can be inherited, or acquired through training and conscious effort. An example of a skill is knowing how to fix a motor or set a broken bone. A competency is more than this – it's a combination of knowledge, skills, and abilities required for achieving results. An example is being a charismatic leader with the ability and know-how to get people to follow you enthusiastically.

There are five important problem-solving competencies. These are drive and initiative, using a methodical approach, teamwork, astute problem analysis, and innovative thinking.

Drive and initiative

To solve problems effectively, you need to take the initiative, tackling new problems energetically and enthusiastically. People with drive and initiative feel confident that they can get things done, and don't get put off by setbacks. They have clear goals in mind and visualize the outcomes they want to see. Plus they are outgoing and able to lead and guide others towards their goals.

Methodical approach

People who are good at problem solving are able

to adopt a methodical, step-by-step approach – and stick to it. They draw on tried-and-tested problem-solving techniques to help them find solutions. At any point in the process, they know where they are and have a clear understanding of what still needs to be done. Rather than trusting subjective emotional responses, they are committed to using logic and reason to work through problems.

Teamwork

Effective problem solvers are good team players. They value different opinions and are able to listen to them with an open mind. They seek out the collaboration of others, and are able to manage and structure discussions so that everyone is able to have their say. When building a team, they counteract the weaknesses of some with the strengths of others. And they encourage open communication between everyone involved.

Astute analysis

Good problem solvers dig deeper to the root causes of problems and reject superficial explanations. They systematically ask probing questions to uncover new information. They remain curious and seek out new advice or clues – and don't discount these even if they appear to contradict other assumptions. They're able to spot patterns or make links to make a situation clearer. Finally, they

64. Problem-Solving and Decision-Making Strategies can describe complicated situations and concepts to others.

Innovative thinking

Innovative thinking is a key competency of effective problem solvers – they constantly search for new ways to approach problems and find solutions. They try different techniques to determine which are best. They see each problem as one of a kind, with unique features that require fresh, objective analysis. Effective problem-solvers also remain open to their own intuitive, creative thought processes.

Question

Marco has a reputation as an excellent problem solver.

Classify Marco's competencies by matching them to their descriptions.

Options:
A. Drive and initiative
B. Methodical approach
C. Teamwork
D. Astute analysis
E. Innovative thinking

Targets:
1. Marco is a confident and enthusiastic leader
2. Marco is a strategist who systematically

thinks through the consequences of his proposals

3. Marco likes to hear what everyone involved has to say about a problem

4. Marco is hardly ever satisfied with the first explanation he hears

5. Marco loves the challenge of finding unique solutions for each problem he encounters

Answer

People with drive and initiative don't shy away from new problems, but meet them with energy and confidence.

Good problem solvers adopt a methodical approach to problems, thinking them through logically and carefully.

Effective problem solving often relies on teamwork. Team players treat the input of others as vital information. They seek out other opinions and make sure everyone has their say.

Effective problem solvers reject superficial explanations. They analyze situations astutely to dig deeper to the core causes of problems.

Innovative thinking involves approaching each new problem as unique, and not relying on past solutions to apparently similar problems.

Problem Solving: Determining and Building Your Strengths
Assessing Your Problem-solving Styles
Developing Your Problem-solving Skills
Recognizing Bias in Problem Solving

Assessing Your Problem-solving Styles

There are four problem-solving styles: rational, nonlinear, pragmatic, and interpersonal. Each style has strengths and weaknesses, or blind spots.

You can determine your own dominant style by developing a problem-solving style chart. First, you review a few problems you recently solved to discover how you responded to them. You then assign a value from 1 to 5 to each style depending on the extent to which you exhibited it when dealing with the problems. You plot the values on a chart and connect the highest points. Knowing your dominant style can help you identify your blind spots so that you can work to overcome them. Relying on a balance of styles – rather than on any one in particular – is best.

Introducing problem-solving styles

When a team is faced with a problem, one person may focus on analyzing facts. Another may quickly work on a solution that's practical, although it doesn't take all possibilities into account. A third person may favor a group approach, in which everyone's thoughts are considered. And someone else may focus on thinking laterally to come up with a creative solution nobody else would've identified.

Types of problems vary, and people often use a combination of approaches to solve them.

However, each person typically has a dominant problem-solving style – an approach they tend to favor or turn to first when problems arise.

Think about how you generally tackle a problem. Is there an approach you usually favor? For example, do you usually take a methodical approach that involves assessing all the facts? Or do you tend to start with a more creative approach like brainstorming possible solutions?

A person's dominant problem-solving approach depends on many factors – some voluntary and others not. For instance, your typical approach may depend on your past experiences, your personality, the skills you have, and what you believe yourself to be good at. It may also be affected by the education you've had.

Different problem-solving styles can be grouped into four main types: rational, nonlinear, pragmatic, and interpersonal. No one of these approaches is always better than the others. Each has both advantages and disadvantages.

Rational

People with a predominantly rational style favor an analytical, structured approach to problem solving. They like to work with the facts of a situation and approach problems objectively.

Nonlinear

A nonlinear style is characterized by creative and original thinking. People who employ this style are able to conceptualize a situation. They are intellectually driven and have vision.

Pragmatic

A pragmatic style is a practical, goal-oriented approach to problem solving. People with this style focus on finding quick, workable solutions. They may appear confident and have a reputation for getting things done efficiently.

Interpersonal

Someone with a predominantly interpersonal style approaches problems collaboratively, relying on interpersonal communication and the company

64. Problem-Solving and Decision-Making Strategies

and opinions of others. This is the most emotional and spontaneous style – friends, family, and colleagues may influence the decisions reached.

A disadvantage to relying on one style over others is that this can lead to blind spots. You may fail to see potential determining factors in a situation, and you may overlook a potential solution.

Those with a rational approach may find the most logical or well-considered solutions to problems. However, they may also be indecisive, overcautious, overly analytical, and rigid in their thinking.

For example, if your approach is strictly rational, you may get bogged down by looking at what's on paper. You may also be limited to what has been tried before, and miss the opportunity to find a creative, new approach to solving a problem.

The blind spots for people who favor the nonlinear style are that they tend to be unrealistic or impractical, disorganized in their approach to problem solving, and occasionally naive. Their ability to think out-of-the box may produce innovative solutions, but these may not be compatible with realities such as nonnegotiable budgets or schedules.

Pragmatists have blind spots too. Their

dedication to finding a practical resolution to a problem may lead them to be short-sighted or impulsive in devising solutions. Because they know they can get things done efficiently and focus on finding solutions without being distracted, they may disregard the interpersonal aspects of problem-solving, and overlook colleagues' opinions.

People with an interpersonal approach to problem solving may be seen as fair and sensitive to others. But they may also be impulsive or sentimental. They may personalize situations and lose their objectivity.

If you rush to find a solution that others agree on, it's likely you'll overlook facts. This can mean spending time and money on implementing a response that's ineffective – or that works only over the short term.

Question

What do you think is the benefit of identifying your own dominant problem-solving style?

Options:

1. Once you know your dominant style, you can rely on it to overcome problems
2. Identifying your dominant style makes it easier to assess your strengths and weaknesses
3. Identifying your dominant style will provide

64. Problem-Solving and Decision-Making Strategies you with a clear indication of your personality type

Answer

Option 1: This option is incorrect. Relying too much on a particular problem-solving style can lead to blind spots and limit your effectiveness.

Option 2: This is the correct option. Knowing your dominant problem-solving style can help you recognize where your strengths and weaknesses lie so that you can take steps to improve the way you approach and solve problems. It will alert you to the types of blind spots you should focus on addressing.

Option 3: This option is incorrect. Your dominant problem-solving style may be partially determined by your personality, but other factors – like your education and history – also play a role. The purpose of identifying your style should be to improve your effectiveness in solving problems.

Identifying your dominant style

Once you're able to identify the characteristics and blind spots of each of the four problem-solving styles, you can determine your own dominant style by creating a problem-solving style chart. Knowing your dominant style can help you identify and then address your weaknesses.

You can create your own chart by using **five steps**:

1. review a few problems you recently solved to uncover the impetus and reasoning behind your actions

2. when reviewing the problems, assign each style a value from 1 to 5 depending on how you used it in solving the problem, then plot the points on the chart

3. connect the points that represent the highest values of each style 4. identify the dominant style you used, and

5. identify possible blind spots

Janet is a human resources manager working at Blazerfire, a publishing company specializing in self- help books. It recently ventured into the publication of cook books. Janet wants to become a better problem solver so you decide to help her create her own problem-solving style chart.

64. Problem-Solving and Decision-Making Strategies

There are four problems Janet recently needed to address related to the company's expansion plans: Should I use online recruiters to search for a cook book editor? Should we adopt a telecommuting arrangement with the editorial staff? Who should facilitate the training for editorial assistants? Where should the company hold this year's annual stakeholder meeting?

Now you have to consider the way Janet addressed her problems and rate her thinking according to each of the four problem-solving styles. This is a very subjective process – you'll need to make judgment calls. A rating of 1 indicates a subordinate style, whereas a rating of 5 indicates a dominant style.

You begin the process by considering how Janet answered her first question – Should I use online recruiters? Over time, she has established a large contact base among all types of recruiters through regular interaction with contributors and readers of human resources newsletters. She's also joined a human resources chat room to keep up to date with the latest industry trends. So she plans to use these channels to help her recruit.

Interpersonal
Janet's approach rested heavily on her

communication skills with others so you rate the interpersonal style a 5.

Rational

You score Janet a 2 on the rational style because she tended to rely heavily on other people's opinions – not facts.

Nonlinear

Rather than thinking creatively herself, Janet relied on the information given to her by creative thinkers she knows. You therefore assign the nonlinear style a rating of 2.

Pragmatic

You score Janet a low 1 on the pragmatic style, because she expressed that she enjoyed the experience of interacting more than achieving the actual goal.

When Janet addressed her second problem – Should we adopt a telecommuting arrangement with the editorial staff? – she became passionate about the topic because the employees who were already telecommuting had told her it had given them the work-life balance they were hoping for. Telecommuting can be a daring arrangement for a company to make, but she was not very concerned about logistical issues because she felt that the positive effect on morale would be well worth it.

64. Problem-Solving and Decision-Making Strategies

So you rate Janet a 5 on the use of the interpersonal style, a 3.5 on the use of the nonlinear style, and a 1 on the use of the pragmatic style.

However, when considering the question of telecommuting, Janet also took the time to review other perspectives and factors, and realized that telecommuting may make certain team-based tasks more difficult to complete. So you rate her a 2 on rational.

Question

You've assigned a value and plotted the points on the problem-solving style chart for two of the four problems that Janet resolved.

Which do you think is the dominant style used by Janet so far in this scenario?

On Janet's problem-solving style chart, the ratings in the rational column are 2 and 2. The ratings in the nonlinear column are 2 and 3.5. In the pragmatic column, the ratings are 1 and 1. And in the interpersonal column, the ratings are 5 and 5.

Options:
1. Rational
2. Nonlinear
3. Pragmatic
4. Interpersonal

Answer

Sorin Dumitrascu

Considering the responses to the first two questions, the interpersonal style is the dominant style because a score of 5 for both proves that Janet relies heavily on it. All the other styles have lower ratings.

So far, the interpersonal style is the dominant style. To see if this trend holds, you continue assigning values based on how Janet resolved the third and fourth problems.

To address the third problem – Who should facilitate the training for editorial assistants? – Janet decided to try a truly innovative approach and poll all the editors for their personal views on local training facilitators, then make a hiring selection based on their input. You score her a 5 on the nonlinear style and a 4.5 on the interpersonal style.

While she didn't crunch the numbers or consider the drawbacks to the polling approach, Janet believed that a good trainer would be cost beneficial in the long run because the new assistants would receive superb training. In other words, she was goal-oriented in her approach, but not very analytical, so you score her a 3 on the pragmatic style and a 1 on the rational style.

Finally, you consider how Janet answered the question "Where should the company hold the

64. Problem-Solving and Decision-Making Strategies

stakeholder meeting?" She knew that the budget for that meeting had been cut, so she reduced the list of possible venues. However, she wanted all managers to have a say in the decision, so she provided them with the list and asked them to vote for their favorite destination.

For this approach, you gave Janet a score of 4 on the interpersonal, a 3.5 on the rational, a 2.5 on the pragmatic, and a 1 on the nonlinear style.

Once you've rated the way Janet responded to her problems according to each of the problem-solving styles, you can connect the highest values of each of the four styles.

Clearly, the trend continued and Janet's dominant style remained the interpersonal style. Although she was comfortable with the nonlinear style, the interpersonal style logged two ratings of 5, while the nonlinear style logged only one rating of 5. Also, on average, she used the interpersonal style most frequently in her problem solving.

But what were Janet's blind spots? Not all problems lend themselves to the interpersonal approach. Dealing with budget issues, for example, often requires an analytical, instead of an emotional approach. She may need to adopt a more objective and rational strategy when those types of issues arise.

Another problem with favoring the interpersonal style is that it may come across as overly personal or sentimental. This style also focuses heavily on interpersonal communication, which is open to misunderstandings.

Question

Nancy has just completed a problem-solving style chart. According to her chart, which statements describe her dominant style and blind spots?

On Nancy's problem-solving style chart, the ratings in the rational column are 4, 3, 4.5, and 5. The ratings in the nonlinear column are 1,1, 3, and 1.5. In the pragmatic column the ratings are 2.5, 2, 3. and 3.5. And in the interpersonal column, they are 1.5, 0.5, 3.5, and 1.5.

Options:

1. Nancy approaches problems analytically
2. Nancy prefers to discover solutions in a team
3. Nancy's style can be disorganized because she likes to use innovative solutions
4. Nancy may appear uncreative and rigid in her problem solving

Answer

Option 1: This is a correct option. The highest scores are situated in the chart's rational column, which indicates that Nancy's dominant style is

64. Problem-Solving and Decision-Making Strategies

analytical and objective.

Option 2: This is an incorrect option. Nancy tends to use the rational style more often than the interpersonal. She's therefore more likely to prefer an analytical than a highly collaborative approach.

Option 3: This is an incorrect option. Nancy's high score on the rational style indicates she's highly structured and analytical, and therefore not disorganized. Her blind spots are that she's too analytical and cautious when finding a solution to a problem.

Option 4: This is a correct option. Nancy's scores indicate she prefers a rational approach to an interpersonal or creative approach, so she may come across as uncreative, uncaring, and inflexible at times.

Developing Your Problem-solving Skills

Different problem-solving styles depend on different problem-solving skills, including analytical, creative, and practical skills. Analytical skills encompass logic, reason, and abstract thinking, whereas creative skills relate to the ability to devise innovative solutions. Practical skills are those used when solving situational problems using your experience and intuition.

To improve analytical skills, get into the habit of asking questions to analyze your problems and solutions. Also engage in text analysis, Socratic thinking, and critical thinking exercises.

Creative thinking can be enhanced by allowing for the saturation, incubation, and illumination of ideas; thinking outside the box; using existing ideas for alternative purposes; and incorporating randomness into your thinking about a problem.

Problem-solving skills

More often than not, the problem-solving style you adopt will depend, at least in part, on your problem- solving skills. In other words, you'll tend to favor the type of approach you're best equipped to use. There are three main types of problem-solving skills – analytical, creative, and practical. Each has a specific role in effective problem solving.

Analytical skills involve the use of logic, reason, and abstract thinking to solve problems, based on available information. Creative skills are generally used in solving problems that are new and unfamiliar. And practical skills are those you apply when solving situational problems that arise as part of everyday life.

Analytical

An analytical approach to problem solving is rational, linear, and logical. It involves addressing a problem by assessing hard data and asking questions. For example, what is the nature of the problem, what is the goal in addressing it, and what are the possible solutions and their pros and cons? What steps must be taken to implement the best solution, and what is the outcome?

Critical thinking is the main skill required for

this approach.

Creative

A creative approach to problem solving focuses on the creation of unusual ideas and solutions that are unique to specific problems. Businesses today rely on innovation to remain competitive, so there's high demand for creativity and thinking "outside of the box."

The starting point for creative problem solving is realizing that the possibility of a novel or atypical solution exists. Then you need to clear your mind of the normal – or typical – approaches and theories. This is how you allow your imagination to run free so that you can come up with unusual, original solutions.

Practical

A practical approach to problem solving involves relying on your experience and intuition to solve problems as they arise. It requires a willingness to tackle existing difficulties, and to use trial and error when necessary. It also requires that you don't over-react emotionally to problems, but instead focus on finding pragmatic solutions.

Practical problem-solving skills don't depend on your level of education or require a lot of functional analysis or critical thinking. Instead they rely on experience and adaptability. Organizations should

64. **Problem-Solving and Decision-Making Strategies** encourage practical skills by recognizing, institutionalizing, and rewarding any practical thinking on the job.

Analytical and creative skills are those that can be specifically built up and honed. However, all three types of skills are important in problem-solving situations.

Just as there are many types of problems, there can be many possible solutions to a single problem. These can evolve from analytical, creative, and practical approaches.

Being able to use your skills effectively to solve problems doesn't assist you only in overcoming obstacles or reaching goals. It also has emotional benefits. It can build your self-confidence and satisfaction in the work you do. In turn, this can make you an even better and more flexible problem solver.

It's important to be aware of the problem-solving skills you have and those you don't. Knowing what your weak areas are is useful when you're trying to develop your skills.

When identifying the skills you want to develop, you should take several factors into account. These include your aptitude, the business environment you work in, your career, and your talents and needs.

This helps ensure that the problem-solving skills you aim to develop are those that will be really useful to you.

One method of evaluating your weak areas is to construct a "Mr/Ms Perfect Problem Solver" profile, a composite problem solver based on several people you consider to be good problem solvers. Jot the names of these individuals down and, next to each name, make a note of the skills they have that impress you most.

An alternative to this method of assessing your weaker areas is to use a problem-solving style chart. Generally, you'll find that analytical skills are associated predominantly with the rational and pragmatic problem-solving styles. Creative skills are associated more with the nonlinear and interpersonal styles.

Question

You'd like to evaluate your problem-solving skills so that you can determine which areas you need to work on improving.

In which ways is it effective to do this?

Options:

1. After creating a composite of several admired problem-solvers' skills, change your style to emulate theirs

64. Problem-Solving and Decision-Making Strategies

2. After identifying the skills you'd like to improve, assess whether they align to your needs, aptitudes, and career path

3. Think about what you're already good at and work on refining the relevant skills

4. Take time out to assess the problem-solving skills of people you consider to be good problem solvers

5. Identify the lowest-scoring styles on your problem-solving style chart, and work on improving skills associated with these

Answer

Option 1: This option is incorrect. Although you can use the model of a "Mr/Ms Perfect Problem Solver," it's unrealistic to emulate that hypothetical person. Instead, focus on what's realistic or possible, and on skills useful in your specific situation.

Option 2: This option is correct. When setting a goal of improving certain problem-solving skills, you should take your aptitudes, needs, and career path into account. This will lead to greater success in your attempts to improve your skills, and ensure you focus on skills that are useful and relevant to you.

Option 3: This option is incorrect. It is important to take your aptitudes into account when you decide which skills to target in your improvement efforts.

However, it's generally skills in your weak areas that you should focus on improving.

Option 4: This option is correct. Considering the skills of various people you consider to be good problem solvers can help you identify the skills you'd most like to develop yourself.

Option 5: This option is correct. Using a problem-solving style chart can assist you in identifying which areas you're weaker and stronger in. In turn, this can help you determine which types of skills to focus on improving.

Improving analytical skills

To improve your analytical skills, you need to enhance your critical thinking. But what does this involve?

In practice, critical thinking involves asking as many questions as possible to analyze all the possible solutions to a problem. Simply making critical thinking a habit can improve your ability to be analytical.

Your education may also have given you a strong foundation for critical thinking because this type of thinking can be developed through practice.

Analytical thinking is used throughout the six-step problem-solving process. The key aspects of problem solving that are affected by your ability to think critically include problem formulation, the assessment of proposed solutions, and solution implementation.

Problem formulation

It's common to mistake the symptoms of problems for problems themselves. It takes critical thinking to identify what a problem really is and to uncover its root causes.

Asking "why" successively can help you uncover root causes. For instance, the answer to

"Why are we short on inventory this month?" might be "Because we sold more stock than we ordered." "Why did we sell more than we ordered? Because we used last year's numbers to make this year's projections." "Why did we do that? Because we lack a precise model for making projections." This kind of persistent questioning can reveal surprising root causes and suggest timely solutions.

You also need to think critically to determine the desired result of addressing the problem. Ask yourself what conditions the solution must satisfy to be considered effective.

Proposed solutions

Once you're familiar with the nature of a problem, you need to think critically to formulate possible solutions – and to analyze each of these.

Use the data that's available to assess the risks and benefits associated with each potential solution. And if possible, discuss the various alternatives you've identified, and their risks and effects, with colleagues or a mentor.

When evaluating solutions, it's useful to ask questions such as "What is my goal and how will this solution help me achieve my goal?" "How will this solution impact individuals who are involved?" "What is the expected return on investment of each solution?" and "How acceptable is each solution to

64. Problem-Solving and Decision-Making Strategies
various stakeholders?"

Solution implementation

When you've decided which solution is best for solving a problem, you need to put it into practice. At this stage, it's essential that you assess the solution critically as it's being implemented. This is because it's vital to ensure that the chosen solution is really effective in solving the problem.

To evaluate the success of a solution, you can ask questions such as "Is the solution having satisfactory effects?" and "Am I comfortable to leave the situation and move on to other matters?"

To practice and develop your critical thinking, you should make sure that you expose yourself to occasions that call for it.

Those who deal with information, system, or text analysis, or whose jobs involve researching or editing, often have to think critically on a daily basis. But even if you're not in any of these fields, various exercises can assist you in building your critical thinking skills.

Three main strategies – or types of exercises – can help you develop your critical thinking skills:
- text analysis, which involves analyzing or comparing text,
- Socratic thinking, which involves specific

- questioning that encourages thinking, and
- critical thinking exercises such as puzzles and questions that stimulate analytical thinking.

Text analysis

Text analysis can involve identifying specific issues or points of interest in text, explaining their significance and your thoughts surrounding them, and identifying how the points are related.

Alternatively, it may involve comparing different texts on a similar subject to determine their relationships – where they converge and where they agree.

In both cases, text analysis requires close attention to content and critical thinking.

Socratic thinking

Socratic thinking refers to the disciplined use of questioning to explore complex issues, concepts, theories, or problems. It typically involves analyzing a multifaceted issue or problem, or a hypothetical situation. It's also useful in differentiating between what is fact and what is pure assumption.

Educators often use Socratic thinking exercises to explore students' knowledge of a particular subject matter and to encourage analytical thought.

64. Problem-Solving and Decision-Making Strategies

Critical thinking exercises

Exercises such as questions and puzzles promote creative and critical thinking. Brain teasers and logic puzzles are good examples.

Brain teasers encourage both critical thought and close attention to detail. Number puzzles such as Sudoku or nonograms such as Pic-a-Pix are logic puzzles that generally require a process of elimination based on reasoning.

Question

Which activities or lines of questioning will help you sharpen your analytical skills?

Options:

1. Asking "What conditions must the solution satisfy in order to be considered successful?"

2. Engaging in methodical thinking and questioning about complex issues and theories

3. Asking "Is it possible to find someone else who knows how to solve this problem?"

4. Approaching the problem from a creative point of view, developing a solution that's not conventional

5. Challenging your thinking by engaging in logic puzzles such as Mathdoku or Soduko

Answer

Option 1: This option is correct. In the problem

formulation stage it's important to determine what the conditions are that the solution must satisfy. Socratic thinking – which involves questioning that encourages thinking – helps you to do this and is therefore a way to sharpen your analytical skills.

Option 2: This option is correct. Engaging in methodical, disciplined questioning about complex issues is an example of Socratic thinking, and this helps develop analytical skills.

Option 3: This is an incorrect option. In order to sharpen analytical skills, it's essential that you engage in the specific problem and its resolution. Attempting to "pass the buck" will not help you develop your problem-solving skills.

Option 4: This option is incorrect. Although this is one way of solving a problem, it's not an analytical method. Analytical skills encompass methodical, well thought out steps to develop a solution, rather than looking for the unconventional, creative solution.

Option 5: This is a correct option. Logic puzzles such as Mathdoku or Sudoko get you to solve problems by working through a process of elimination based on reasoning. This is a good way to improve your analytical skills.

Improving creative skills

Just as you can use exercises to develop analytical skills, you can use specific strategies to improve and refine your creative problem-solving skills. The first of these involves allowing for the saturation, incubation, and illumination of ideas.

Saturation

To think creatively, you need to tap into the knowledge you've accumulated over many years. If you restrict yourself to thinking logically and rationally, this could stifle your ability to think creatively.

Your aim at this stage is to saturate your mind with all sorts of information about the problem. To devise a creative solution, you need to delve into, sift through, and use this information. The process of saturation involves filling your mind with all the knowledge about a problem that's at your disposal.

Incubation

Incubation relies on your stepping back from a problem and allowing your mind to focus on something else. You should let your mind continue to process the problem and its specifics, but not at a conscious level that involves too much effort.

Often, suspending your rigorous thinking about a

problem by taking a break from it and engaging in something unrelated will give your brain an opportunity to "incubate" – or develop – creative ideas. Temporarily stepping away from a problem can allow the creative part of your brain to continue working on it.

Illumination

The illumination of ideas refers to bringing them to light, or uncovering them. It is the "Aha!" or "Eureka!" moment when a creative solution first occurs to you. Often this occurs while you are engaged in something totally unrelated to the problem – cooking, talking, even sleeping!

Of course, not every creative idea will be feasible. Once you've uncovered creative ideas for approaching a problem, you need to validate them to confirm that they're realistic and appropriate.

A second strategy for improving your creative thinking is to practice thinking "outside the box." This simply refers to viewing things from another perspective. It involves challenging or overcoming the conventional ways in which you think, because these limit your ability to approach problems creatively.

One way of getting into the habit of thinking outside the box is to question what's conventional,

64. Problem-Solving and Decision-Making Strategies

or simply accepted. You might ask questions like "Is there another way?" or "Why can't we...?" Sometimes there's a very good business reason why a particular approach has been accepted as convention, but at other times, questioning can lead to innovative thinking and better solutions.

Lateral-thinking exercises can also encourage creative thinking. In one famous dot puzzle, for example, you need to connect all the dots using four straight lines but without lifting your pen from the paper.

The only way to solve this puzzle is to draw the lines outside the borders of the square area created by the dots. So this is a literal example of thinking outside a box.

You can also improve your creative skills by using existing ideas for alternative purposes – building on or adapting them in creative ways.

For instance, the Wright brothers – who are credited with inventing the world's first successful airplane – drew their inspiration and ideas from various other inventors, including Sir George Cayley and Leonardo da Vinci. They took the original ideas of these individuals and used them in different ways to form their own ideas.

Similarly, Albert Einstein built his revolutionary theory of relativity partly on equations that theorist

James Maxwell had proposed to explain electromagnetic fields. By taking the equations a step further than Maxwell did and using them for a purpose that Maxwell had not imagined, Einstein developed a novel, creative theory.

A final strategy for honing your creative skills is to incorporate more randomness in your thinking. Often, finding creative solutions depends on your allowing your mind to process information freely, instead of confining it only to what seem like logical or rational routes.

For instance, you might open a book at a random sentence and consider how it could possibly be used to think about or solve your problem. A random idea might provide just the conceptual jolt you need to trigger an "Aha!" moment.

Question
In which ways can you help sharpen your creative problem-solving skills?
Options:
1. Take some time out to become familiar with the problem by thinking about it and all related knowledge you have
2. Be systematic and logical in your approach to evaluating a problem
3. After giving your problem due thought, make

64. Problem-Solving and Decision-Making Strategies

a conscious effort to persistently keep it in the forefront of your mind

4. Make a point of viewing a problem from different perspectives

5. Build on existing ideas and solutions and think about different ways you can use them 6. Attempt to think of a few random and unconventional solutions to problems

Answer

Option 1: This option is correct. The process of saturation involves filling your mind with a problem and all related knowledge you have about it, without consciously analyzing your thoughts. This can facilitate the creative thought process.

Option 2: This option is incorrect. To sharpen your creative thinking skills, you need to practice thinking more freely – rather than confining your mind to an analytical or strictly logical approach.

Option 3: This option is incorrect. Although it's good to initially saturate your mind with a problem, you should then temporarily step back from it to allow ideas to incubate.

Option 4: This option is correct. Creative thinking often relies on thinking outside the box, which requires that you view problems from different viewpoints and challenge accepted norms.

Option 5: This option is correct. Taking existing

ideas and using them for alternative purposes encourages you to think about and adapt them in a creative manner. This then helps to sharpen your creative thinking skills.

Option 6: This option is correct. Incorporating randomness into your thinking allows your mind to process information freely, so you're not restricted to the normal, predictable way of thinking or problem solving.

Although it's always good to acquire new problem-solving skills, it's also important to refine the skills you already have. You can work on developing and sharpening these skills both individually and collectively within your organization.

Recognizing Bias in Problem Solving

Bias occurs when people allow mental or emotional factors to distort their perceptions. It's the source of most mind traps that prevent effective problem solving. Cognitive bias is caused by faulty information- processing methods, and includes bias that arises through framing, anchoring, the relative availability of different types of information, and overconfidence. Motivational bias arises from people's needs and goals, and includes self-enhancement, need for closure, cooperation, and accountability bias.

To guard against bias in problem solving, you should identify the types of bias common to each problem- solving stage, redesign your problem-solving approach if necessary, watch for evidence of bias throughout your problem-solving process, and counter bias as soon as it arises.

Types of bias

We all come across people who make questionable decisions. Examples could be a manager who routinely awards her favorite team members the best assignments, or a car salesman who recommends a more expensive vehicle because it gives him a bigger commission. What do these people have in common? They've all allowed themselves to fall prey to various forms of bias.

Bias is a widely studied phenomenon in problem-solving research. It involves allowing mental or emotional factors to distort your perception of reality.

This skews the problem-solving process. It can influence the data you choose to gather, your analysis of a problem, the solution you choose, and the way you go about implementing the solution. Ultimately, it's the source of most mind traps people fall into when attempting to solve problems.

There are many categories of bias. Two of the most important are cognitive bias and motivational bias.

Cognitive bias

Cognitive bias is a deviation that occurs when you don't follow rational and predictable methods of

64. Problem-Solving and Decision-Making Strategies
information processing.

Motivational bias

Motivational bias causes people to see things in a way that relates to their own goals or needs – preventing them from seeing things completely objectively.

Your mind can only process a limited amount of information. However, various mental shortcuts – the different types of cognitive bias – help you to raise this limit.

Because these shortcuts introduce bias, your thoughts and actions differ from what can be measured objectively. For example, misjudging the amount of risk presented by a course of action is a common cognitive bias that results from the use of such shortcuts.

Different types of cognitive bias include framing, anchoring, availability, and overconfidence.

Framing refers to the way you present or initially perceive a situation. This can distort your view of the facts.

Positive framing emphasizes possible benefits, whereas negative framing emphasizes possible losses or risks.

The way you frame a situation affects traits such

as risk-taking. For example, say a patient must decide whether to undergo a risky medical treatment for a disease. The patient is more likely to go ahead if told there's a 60% chance of survival than if a doctor frames the risk negatively, as a 40% chance of death.

A phenomenon related to framing bias is task perception bias, which can affect how you interpret problems. This occurs if you allow your view of a situation to be influenced by superficial details, such as the way tasks or processes are named.

For example, researchers found that people behaved more cooperatively when asked to participate in the "community game" than they did when asked to participate in the "Wall Street game," although the games played were identical. The "Wall Street game" was perceived as more competitive.

Anchoring bias occurs when you allow your initial data on a problem to outweigh later information that differs from it. It results from the way you build up ideas – by taking initial values and adding to them as you acquire more data.

This can create bias by causing you to base judgments on a point of reference – or initial value – that is outdated. Anchoring bias can also appear when you allow results obtained in similar but

64. Problem-Solving and Decision-Making Strategies

different situations to influence your decisions.

For example, a study on real-estate agents showed that when given low initial offers for a property, they settled for lower sale prices than when given high initial offers. Their satisfaction with the results they obtained was also influenced by factors such as prevailing market prices, which they had incorporated into their reference points.

The availability bias occurs because you don't process all forms of information equally. How data is presented influences your reaction to it.

Concrete and vivid information is easier to remember – and this can lead you to overestimate its importance. Similarly, you may completely overlook information that's less boldly presented or harder to visualize.

For example, many people overestimate the likelihood of plane crashes – which are vividly portrayed in the media when they occur. But they underestimate the likelihood of car crashes, which are much more common but attract less attention.

A final type of cognitive bias is overconfidence. Being too confident can impair your judgment, leading you to overestimate the likely success of possible solutions and to overlook potential risks.

Research has shown that overconfident problem

solvers are more confrontational, and ignore alternative solutions that could provide better results. They may also fail to provide backup plans because they ignore the possibility of failure or mishaps.

Question

Match each type of cognitive bias to the scenario in which it has occurred.

Options:

A. Framing bias
B. Anchoring bias
C. Availability bias
D. Overconfidence bias

Targets:

1. Tina must decide if she'll gamble on a new product that has a 30% chance of failure. She rejects the product.

2. Jay's choice of vehicles for the company fleet follows his initial idea about the best model – despite later findings showing the model's low fuel efficiency.

3. After Abe's store is robbed for the first time, he hires a security firm to protect the store against what he claims is a local crime wave.

4. Ronald is sure his new sales approach will succeed despite early evidence indicating that it isn't

64. Problem-Solving and Decision-Making Strategies

going well.

Answer

Tina framed the problem negatively, which decreased the amount of risk she was willing to tolerate. Had she viewed it as a 70% chance of success, her decision may have been different.

Jay has anchored himself to his initial idea about which model of vehicle is best – causing him to ignore other information he has found. This leads him to discount other options that could provide better value.

Abe is overestimating the impact of the robbery. Because it was so important to him, he believes it to be part of a bigger trend that requires him to take action. This is an example of bias based on the availability of information.

Ronald is being overconfident – he lacks evidence to support his certainty, and hasn't allowed for the possibility that his approach may fail.

Motivational bias arises because people's approaches to problems are affected by their own goals or needs. It's difficult to guard against motivational bias because it can be difficult to spot.

Types of motivational bias include bias that arises due to people's drive for self-enhancement, their desire for cooperation, their need for closure, and their accountability to others.

Self-enhancement bias

Self-enhancement bias occurs when you choose solutions that maximize your well-being or make you look good, instead of the solutions that address problems most effectively.

For example, you may consciously or even subconsciously favor decisions you know will impress your manager or colleagues. You may also fall into the trap of automatically supporting solutions that you helped create, even if other, better solutions are available.

Cooperation bias

Cooperation bias arises when you focus on finding solutions that will please everyone, in order to avoid jeopardizing future cooperation within a group. Sometimes this goal can bias your judgment and prevent the best possible solution to a problem – which may not please all participants – from being chosen.

Of course, cooperation is a worthy goal in many problem-solving contexts, and often a cooperative solution is the best solution. But allowing cooperation to trump all other factors is a bias that threatens the objectivity of the problem-solving process.

64. Problem-Solving and Decision-Making Strategies

Need for closure bias

It's natural to want to solve problems and move on – and sometimes deadlines mean that solutions are needed quickly. However, a need for closure can create bias by leading you to cut the problem-solving process short.

Working under pressure can cause you to oversimplify complex situations and overlook possible solutions. It can also lead you to ignore innovative thinking in favor of tried and tested routines. This is problematic because previous solutions won't always apply to new problems.

Accountability bias

When you're accountable to others or responsible for their well-being, you're likely to consider information more carefully and to take more care in devising solutions to problems.

However, focusing on your accountability to others can also color your approach to problems. Research shows that people who are accountable for others act more aggressively and uncompromisingly during negotiations, which can cause them to overlook solutions that are fairer for everyone involved.

Wendy and Michael are discussing a project they're collaborating on. Follow along to see how they've allowed motivational bias to influence the problem-solving process.

Wendy: *Michael, we need to get this project done as quickly as possible. Our client has us on a very tight schedule.*

Michael: *Well, you and I could work on fast-tracking the analysis phase. That will mean bringing in more resources, so it will cost the client more – but I know everyone on my team would like the chance to be more involved before the implementation phase starts.*

Wendy: *Maybe we should skip the analysis phase. We already know what the client wants, and it would really impress my boss if we could get this done on time!*

Michael: *If you're sure about it, I guess we could...*

Wendy and Michael have allowed several types of motivational bias to creep into their problem-solving process.

Wendy has cut the problem-solving process short because of a deadline and the need for closure. She also displays signs of self-enhancement bias – she focuses on what her boss will think, rather than on finding the best possible solution.

64. Problem-Solving and Decision-Making Strategies

Michael displayed cooperation bias in choosing a solution that favors himself and Wendy over their client. He also focuses on his accountability to his team, rather than on finding the best possible solution.

Question

Match each type of motivational bias to the scenario in which it's demonstrated.

Options:

A. Self-enhancement bias
B. Cooperation bias
C. Need for closure bias
D. Accountability bias

Targets:

1. Sara pleases her boss by choosing the cheap supplier, though its service is inferior
2. David mediates between two companies and chooses a solution that both favor, even though it will not address the problem in the long run
3. In order to get back on track more quickly after a production breakdown, Kelly skips the analysis sessions and uses an old recovery plan instead
4. Ian's team members are short of cash, so he decides that signing them up for extra overtime is the best solution for completing a project on time

Answer

Sara is showing signs of self-enhancement bias by making a choice that will improve her status instead of one that serves her company best. This is an example of self-enhancement bias.

David is showing cooperation bias by favoring the interests of the people he is dealing with, rather than choosing the better long-term solution.

Kelly's need for problem closure has caused her to cut the problem-solving process short, which could result in errors. Her need for closure has led her to fall back on a solution to a previous problem, and this may not be effective for the new problem she needs to address.

Ian feels accountable to his team members, and so has acted in their interests rather than focusing on finding the best possible solution to a problem.

Recognizing the types of distortions that may creep into your thinking is the first step toward dealing with bias in your problem-solving process.

Question

Bill has been tasked with creating a presentation for a new client. The client's requirements have changed several times, but Bill's presentation is based primarily on the ideas he developed in

64. Problem-Solving and Decision-Making Strategies response to the client's original specifications.

Which type of bias is Bill displaying in this scenario?

Options:
1. Anchoring, which is a cognitive bias
2. Overconfidence, which is a cognitive bias
3. Anchoring, which is a motivational bias
4. Cooperation, which is a motivational bias
5. Overconfidence, which is a motivational bias

Answer

Option 1: This option is correct. Bill continued to use his initial ideas, although the client supplied new information that he should have taken into account. This is an example of anchoring, which is a type of cognitive bias.

Option 2: This option is incorrect. Nothing specifically indicates that Bill is overly confident about the likely success of his presentation, or of the solution he's going to propose.

Option 3: This option is incorrect. Bill is guilty of anchoring bias, but this is a type of cognitive – rather than motivational – bias.

Option 4: This option is incorrect. Bill hasn't specifically allowed his desire to find a solution that will please everyone to bias his judgment of the situation.

Option 5: This option is incorrect. Bill isn't

indicating excessive confidence in his solution. Also, overconfidence is a cognitive bias, rather than a motivational bias.

Handling bias in problem solving

One way of eliminating bias is by following a systematic problem-solving process, like the six-step model.

In addition, you can take specific actions to help prevent bias from skewing the results of the problem- solving process. These include identifying which types of bias are likely to arise during each stage of the process and, when necessary, redesigning your approach to the problem-solving process. They also include watching for evidence of bias and acting to counter any instances of bias you may find.

Identify types of bias likely to arise

Different types of bias are likely to appear at different stages of the problem-solving process. For example, the definition stage of the problem-solving model is vulnerable to framing bias, while the fourth stage – choosing the best solution – can be affected by overconfidence.

Knowing which types of bias to look out for – and when – can help you ensure that the problem-solving process stays objective.

Redesign your approach

Each step of the problem-solving process can be

completed in a variety of ways. So you can redesign the process to help eliminate specific types of bias.

For example, you might choose to ask each member of a team to generate possible solutions to a problem on their own and to submit these anonymously, instead of using a group brainstorming session. This could help prevent both self-enhancement and cooperation bias.

Watch for evidence of bias

It's important that you keep watch for any of the types of bias that can arise during the problem-solving process. This ensures that you can then take action to prevent the process from becoming skewed.

In a team, it's important to ensure all members are aware of the types of bias that can arise and of the negative effects they can have. This will help keep the team vigilant.

Act to counter bias

Once any bias is detected, it's important to take immediate steps to counter it. You can do this by making participants aware that they are demonstrating bias and encouraging them to adjust their thinking appropriately.

For example, you may notice team members falling prey to anchoring bias while analyzing a problem. To rectify the situation, you can point out

64. Problem-Solving and Decision-Making Strategies

the bias and ask the team to begin a new analysis that takes updated information into account.

It can also help to encourage problem solvers to record their ideas and to examine and clarify them.

Taking action to detect and deal with bias will help you keep your problem-solving process as objective as possible.

Question

Which steps can you take to help prevent bias in problem solving?

Options:

1. Identify types of bias likely to arise
2. Redesign your approach
3. Prohibit team members from criticizing any ideas
4. Act to counter bias
5. Identify possible solutions
6. Watch for evidence of bias

Answer

Option 1: This option is correct. Identifying the types of bias likely to arise during each stage of the problem-solving process will help you remain vigilant against the effects of bias.

Option 2: This option is correct. Redesigning your approach to the problem-solving process when necessary can help minimize the occurrence of bias

– for example, by avoiding situations from which bias is likely to arise.

Option 3: This option is incorrect. Closing problem solvers off from opposing views increases the chance of bias creeping into the problem-solving process. Ideas need to be analyzed carefully, and sometimes critiqued.

Option 4: This option is correct. Once bias is detected, it's important to act immediately to counter it. Actions you can take to counter bias include having participants record their ideas so they can be examined and clarified as needed.

Option 5: This option is incorrect. Identifying possible solutions is part of the problem-solving model, rather than a method of countering bias.

Option 6: This option is correct. It's important to keep watch for any signs of bias so that you can act to counter it before it has an impact on the problem-solving process.

Problem Solving: Digging Deeper
Using Fact-based Analysis for Problem Solving
Uncovering the Root Causes
Problem-solving Solutions: Looking Beyond the Obvious

Using Fact-based Analysis for Problem Solving

Fact-based analysis is vital to effective problem solving as it ensures you get to the root cause of the problem and helps you choose the best potential solution to that problem.

There are five fact-based analysis tools: five-why analysis, cause-and-effect diagrams, force-field analysis, cost-benefit analysis, and multi-attribute analysis.

Applying fact-based analysis

If you go to the doctor with a high fever and stomach pain, you would be horrified if she gave you a damp cloth for your head and an antacid and sent you away. Any good doctor would diagnose your illness and prescribe medicine to treat the cause, not the symptoms. The same logic can be applied to problem solving – you need to discover and analyze all the facts so you can identify the true cause. Only then can you search for the best solution.

Fact-based analysis involves studying and dissecting a problem to help you identify the true cause of your problem – and not to wrongly focus your problem-solving efforts on a symptom of the problem. As in the example of the doctor, the symptom of a problem is often different from the cause.

Fact-based analysis also requires you to evaluate potential solutions to ensure you implement the most beneficial one. Without first identifying the true cause of a problem, you might choose a solution that deals only with a symptom. You'll have failed to solve the problem and you'll have wasted resources and time implementing an ineffective solution.

Take the example of a company whose productivity is suffering due to high staff turnover. The HR Department decides that the cause is a new company offering better salaries, so it decides to increase staff salaries by 10% to counter this. However, staff turnover continues to rise. Why? Because lower salaries are not the root cause and are only a symptom of a bigger problem.

It's clear from the example that members of the HR Department failed to analyze the problem to uncover the root cause. This meant their solution wasn't going to be effective. Following the six-step problem- solving model – a flexible step-by-step guide for finding the right solution – would have greatly improved their chances of success.

When analyzing problems and solutions using the problem-solving model, you can choose from a number of tools. So when you analyze a problem in step two, you use either the cause-and-effect diagram or the five-why analysis. And you get help from either the force-field analysis, cost-benefit analysis, or multi-attribute analysis when choosing the best solution in step four.

Five-why analysis

Five-why analysis is an informal and relatively simple tool for determining the root cause of a

64. Problem-Solving and Decision-Making Strategies problem.

Cause-and-effect diagram

You use the cause-and-effect diagram to help you determine all the potential causes of a problem.

Force-field analysis

Force-field analysis is a tool you use to analyze the factors that help or impede a potential solution to a problem.

Cost-benefit analysis

Cost-benefit analysis is a tool for determining the financial payback of a potential solution or plan.

Multi-attribute analysis

You use multi-attribute analysis to compare various solutions to a problem, under a range of different attributes.

These tools are generally used at these specific steps but can be used at other steps too, depending on the situation at hand. These are presented for illustrative purposes and aren't recommendations for real- life problem-solving situations.

Question
What are the benefits of fact-based analysis?
Options:
1. It helps determine the root cause of a problem
2. It solves a problem in the quickest possible

time

3. It ensures you choose the best possible solution to a problem

4. It guarantees the cheapest possible solution to a problem

5. It provides a more effective use of resources

Answer

Option 1: This is a correct option. Using fact-based analysis helps you get to the root cause of a problem. It also means your chosen solution is more likely to be effective.

Option 2: This is an incorrect option. Fact-based analysis helps you get to the root cause of a problem and find an effective solution, regardless of the time it takes.

Option 3: This is a correct option. Fact-based analysis helps you choose the best possible solution to a problem by determining the root cause.

Option 4: This is an incorrect option. Fact-based analysis will help you determine the best possible solution to a problem, regardless of cost.

Option 5: This is a correct option. Fact-based analysis provides a more effective use of resources as time isn't wasted analyzing ineffective alternatives.

Using specific fact-based analysis tools

Five-why analysis uses the simple technique of asking "Why?" until you have moved past the symptoms and discovered the underlying cause of a problem. You begin with an accurate statement of the problem and keep asking why until you get to the root cause. Each question builds on the previous answer, and the technique generally takes five questions but can take more or less.

One drawback to this tool is that it can result in people only pursuing a single path of inquiry. If a question yields multiple answers, you should ask "Why?" of each one and pursue each path to its logical conclusion.

On the plus side, this tool is quick and effective and can be used in almost any situation, from business to home life.

Take the example of a problem statement and how the five-why analysis is applied to it: "We frequently miss delivery deadlines to a certain client." The first question is to ask why the deadlines are missed. The answer is that jobs are going to print too late. The next question builds on this answer and asks why jobs are late going to print. This line of questioning continues until the final question establishes the root cause of the late deliveries: poor communication between two departments.

A cause-and-effect diagram – also known as a fishbone diagram because of its appearance – helps you identify the main causes of a problem and the most important areas in which to search for a solution. It is ideally drawn up in a brainstorming session. First you write down the problem and draw a horizontal line with an arrow pointing toward it. You add "connect" branches that contain main categories of potential causes. Finally, you add causes associated with each category and determine how they affect the problem.

A local police department uses a cause-and-effect diagram to determine how it can improve its slow response time to emergency calls. The problem-solving team writes down the problem statement on a whiteboard and then adds the categories that influence response times: equipment, people, methods, and environment.

Next the team brainstorms various causes linked to each category. One of the causes it identifies is the lack of squad cars. The team lead adds this as a cause to the diagram and links it to the equipment category. The team continues until it has identified a wide range of contributing causes of the slow

64. Problem-Solving and Decision-Making Strategies

response times.

The team then adds causes to the original causes until it has explored every possibility. The benefits of this approach are that the team shares its knowledge and variety of insights and that it discovers multiple causes for a single problem.

You use force-field analysis to evaluate potential solutions to a problem by listing the factors that support or work against the potential solution. You write down the current situation and proposed solution, and then brainstorm all the forces that impact on it – driving forces that work for the solution and restraining forces that work against it. You can then discover which ones can be either strengthened or eliminated to make the solution work.

Consider the example of a small-town cinema. A team has been assembled to boost dwindling attendance. The team decides to use force-field analysis. As a solution, team members propose giving away T-shirts and posters at screenings. The team must now brainstorm the various factors involved.

Some of the driving forces are the fact that the cinema already receives promotional T-shirts from distributors and that some staff are willing to take on extra hours to distribute the merchandise. The restraining forces reveal that the cinema will need to foot the bill for posters to give away, extra staff will inevitably need to be hired, and the free T-shirts advertise the distributor's films, not the cinema itself.

Evaluating the forces leads the team to conclude that while giveaways may attract more customers, the cost of hiring new staff and printing posters outweighs the gain.

Team members now use force-field analysis to compare every solution they've developed to counter poor attendance. They do this until they find an effective solution. After the team implements a plan of action, team members can also measure the results against the forces listed.

You can't use the force-field analysis to discover causes for a problem, nor should you use it in situations with multiple or interconnected problems. It works best when it's focused on a single issue.

Cost-benefit analysis judges a proposed plan of action purely by its financial potential. You'd use it in business when proposing a plan that requires funds, but it can also be used to weigh up the financial gain of an expenditure.

Cost-benefit analysis involves listing all the

64. Problem-Solving and Decision-Making Strategies

costs and financial benefits of your plan, assigning values to each, and then balancing them out to get an end figure. You can also divide the total benefit figure by the total cost figure to get the return value for every unit of currency spent.

It can be difficult to put a price tag on something that may only save money over a period of time, or provide secondary benefits that save money in areas unrelated to your planned purchase, so you need to work out a reasonable estimate to include in your analysis.

Suppose you use a cost-benefit analysis to determine the financial potential of buying a new piece of construction machinery. You first list its cost, the projected maintenance and running costs, and the operator's salary. Next you list the benefits, including a projection of revenue the machine will generate and the resale value of the machine it's replacing. You add up the costs and the benefits, and divide the total benefit by the total cost. The result is the payback value per dollar spent.

Multi-attribute analysis is a tool you use to evaluate multiple solutions against weighted criteria. Criteria are the standards used to evaluate a solution, like cost and feasibility. When you weigh criteria, you assign each a value relative to the others. This allows you to conclude, for example, that cost is three times more important than feasibility.

This tool is similar to cost-benefit analysis because it arrives at a numerical result. However, it takes into account more than simply money. It can include quantitative, qualitative, and normative criteria within a single chart.

Say you are the head of a hospital that's losing many of its highly trained staff. You assemble a team to draw up various solutions to this problem and brainstorm all their advantages and disadvantages. From this list, you determine the criteria to evaluate the solutions.

Once you know your essential criteria, you evaluate them to come up with a numerical value. For example, you decide that cost is worth three times as much as ease of implementation. You then evaluate the solutions against every criterion, scored on a common scale, and then multiply them by the weight. You then add the totals, which gives each solution a score in terms of desirability. In this case, increasing salaries to retain staff is the most desirable solution.

Question

Match each fact-based analysis tool to the

64. Problem-Solving and Decision-Making Strategies example that it would work best with.

Options:
A. Five-why analysis
B. Cause-and-effect diagrams
C. Force-field analysis
D. Cost-benefit analysis
E. Multi-attribute analysis

Targets:
1. To compare different plans for community upliftment, considering cost, time, effect, and feasibility
2. To make a presentation outlining the financial gains that a server upgrade provides
3. To find out which factors will and which ones won't support your plan for a computer upgrade
4. To find the potential causes for all job losses in the transport industry of a certain city
5. To find the root cause to the problem of overspending in the Marketing Department

Answer

To compare different solutions or plans against varying criteria, you use a multi-attribute analysis.

To present the financial gains of a plan or solution, you use a cost-benefit analysis.

To examine the factors that affect a proposed plan, you use a force-field analysis.

To discover multiple causes for a single problem, you use a cause-and-effect diagram.

Sorin Dumitrascu

To discover a single underlying cause for a problem, you use five-why analysis.

Uncovering the Root Causes

Analyzing a problem is most effective when you first identify potential causes, determine the most likely cause, and then dig deeper to identify the root cause.

This can be done using a five-why analysis. This tool involves stating the problem clearly, then asking a series of "Why?" questions based on each answer to peel away the layers and find the true, underlying cause of the problem.

The five-why analysis

In the six-step problem-solving model, the second step is to analyze the problem. The aim of this step is to uncover the root cause of the problem. It's important not to assume that you know what this cause is. Instead you need to dig deeper to avoid dealing with the mere symptoms of a more fundamental, underlying problem.

The second step is about gathering and sorting through information about the problem – after all, there might be several possible causes. Analyzing this information is most effective when you follow certain key sub-steps. You should identify potential causes, determine the most likely cause or causes, and then identify the true root cause or causes of the problem.

i) Identify potential causes

Although a single root cause may exist, a combination of factors could also be contributing to the problem. If you list as many possible causes as you can, you'll have more information to work with. Types of causes that contribute to the problem include materials, people, methods, environmental factors, and so on.

ii) Determine the most likely cause

64. Problem-Solving and Decision-Making Strategies

Next you determine the causes that contribute most to the problem. If you're working with a team, try giving each possibility a score to establish which ranks the highest.

iii) Identify the true root cause

Then you analyze the most likely causes to reveal a root cause. That way, you can prevent the same problems from surfacing again in the future by identifying – and solving – the true underlying cause once and for all.

There are two tools you can use to analyze a problem. One is the cause-and-effect diagram, which you use to map out the various complex causes contributing to the current problem.

The second tool is five-why analysis. While both tools are useful, this course will focus on the second tool because it's the quickest and most straightforward way to get to the root of a problem.

Five-why analysis has a few simple steps you take to get to an underlying cause of a problem. You need to state the problem clearly, and then ask a question about the problem starting with "Why?" You then continue to ask "Why?" of each successive answer until no further answer is apparent. So the final question should reveal and allow you to recognize the root cause of the problem.

1. State the problem clearly

The first, crucial step is to state the problem clearly. This means defining the problem explicitly so it's clear how it is a problem for you and why you want the situation to change. This step doesn't involve trying to provide a complex, overall picture of the situation. You'll only develop it with each successive layer of questioning.

Putting the problem into words helps you ask the right questions about it. If you're working with a team, it's a good idea to write down the problem so you can stay focused on it.

2. Ask a question about the problem

The next step is to ask the question that reveals the cause of the problem. This is the first layer. It's important that you stay focused on the issue and don't get sidetracked by assuming you know what the cause is, asking an unfocused question, or asking about something that you can't measure or observe.

3. Continue to ask "Why?"

Often, the first answer won't reveal the root cause of the problem. After you've found your initial, superficial reason, you ask a "Why?" question about that statement.

Then you ask a question about each successive

64. Problem-Solving and Decision-Making Strategies

answer as many times as you need to until no answer is returned. It could take more or less than five questions to dig to the root cause, depending on the complexity of your problem.

4. Recognize the root cause

When you reach a statement that can't really be followed up with another "Why?" question, you've reached the root cause of the problem. You should beware of stopping too soon and addressing only a symptom of the problem.

If you're working with a team, it's useful to get consensus on whether to stop at the cause you've identified.

Question

What's involved in conducting a five-why analysis?

Options:

1. Ask a "Why?" question about the problem and then ask a series of "Why?" questions to find the root cause

2. Put the problem into precise terms and then ask a series of "Why?" questions until the fundamental cause is revealed

3. Define the problem by finding the root cause of it and then ask a series of "Why?" questions to find a solution

Answer

Option 1: This is an incorrect option. It is crucial to first state the problem clearly to allow you to ask the right questions about it.

Option 2: This is the correct option. First you define the problem. You then dig deeper by asking questions to uncover each layer of causes until you find the root of the problem.

Option 3: This is an incorrect option. You can't find the root cause of a problem before asking questions about it to reveal each layer of causes.

Applying a five-why analysis

You work for a cross-country franchise that manufactures its own brand of outdoor adventure clothing and accessories. Questionnaires filled out by customers at various branches indicate that they are unhappy with sales service at the stores. At a meeting called to address the problem, your team decides to use a five-why analysis to get to the root of the problem.

The first thing your team does is state the problem clearly and simply. That way everyone can agree on what the problem is and keep focused on it.

The first question your team asks about the problem must point to something observable. Asking "Why is customer satisfaction low with our service?" is better than asking "Why don't customers like our service?" because there is no way to observe what people think.

Depending on the complexity of the problem, you may need more than one line of questioning. This allows you to focus on each potential cause of the problem. In this case, your team identifies two possible causes of the problem.

Your team decides to probe the fact that employees don't effectively respond to queries. You do this by asking "Why aren't employees responding to customers' product-related queries in a satisfactory manner?"

This is a good, logical response to the statement, and it allows you to stay focused on the issue and move forward in a systematic way.

Avoid getting off track by asking questions that point to another issue that comes to mind. So at this point, you wouldn't ask "Why are some of our products inferior?" or "Why isn't Jack at this meeting?" because these don't address the issue at hand.

You should also avoid addressing earlier statements. So don't rephrase an earlier question by asking "Why are customers rating our service so low?" because it won't be building the discussion.

The team learns that employees have inadequate knowledge about the product line and therefore can't respond to queries satisfactorily.

The next logical question is to ask why product knowledge is inadequate.

The team discovers that employees don't receive any product training whatsoever.

One team member thinks this is the root cause and votes to stop the discussion. He wants to talk about implementing the employee training program. But the rest of the team decides to go further by asking why current employees aren't receiving

64. Problem-Solving and Decision-Making Strategies training.

The team finds out the company lacks any induction or on-the-job training programs for employees.

Logically, the next question will probe why the company doesn't offer new employees on-the-job training programs to bring product knowledge up to date.

Your team discovers that up until two years ago, all employees were trained on existing and new product lines to ensure everyone remained knowledgeable. However, the training budget was recently cut, and as a result, product knowledge has suffered. This is the root cause of the problem.

How many "Why?" questions you ask will depend on the complexity of the problem. Sometimes one or two questions will get to the root cause. Other times you may need to ask "Why?" many more times.

You'll probably instinctively recognize the root cause statement when you reach it. Otherwise a good rule of thumb is to stop when you can't get more information by asking another "Why?" question, or when your team agrees that it's found the root cause.

Question

Your team is brainstorming to uncover the root cause of a problem. Your problem statement is "The company has lost 25% of its employees over the previous three years."

What is the appropriate response when performing the five-why analysis?

Options:

1. Why have we lost such a high number of employees?

2. How can we encourage employees to stay?

3. Is this a problem with the HR Department?

4. Are employees leaving because competitors offer better salaries?

Answer

Option 1: This is the correct option. This question is a logical response to the problem statement. It probes the problem and points to a more focused answer.

Option 2: This is an incorrect option. This question doesn't attempt to probe the problem. You need to identify the root cause before you can analyze a potential solution.

Option 3: This is an incorrect option. This question shifts focus away from the problem and is attempting to place the blame somewhere else. Instead you need to focus on why employees are leaving.

64. Problem-Solving and Decision-Making Strategies

Option 4: This is an incorrect option. You can't take short cuts by assuming you know what the problem is. Instead, ask a question that reveals the cause of the high turnover.

Question

The first question reveals that a considerable percentage of those who leave are taking similar positions with a competitor.

What's the most appropriate response?

Options:

1. Why are employees taking similar roles elsewhere?
2. Why are employees leaving in such high numbers?
3. How can we compete with the other company?

Answer

Option 1: This is the correct option. This question builds on the previous answer and explores why employees are taking similar positions with a competitor. This question should bring you one step closer to revealing the root cause of the problem.

Option 2: This is an incorrect option. This question doesn't build on the previous answer. To reveal the root cause, you need to stay focused and ask questions that further explore the answer.

Option 3: This is an incorrect option. This question isn't focused and is attempting to come up with a solution before uncovering the root cause.

Question

During employee exit interviews, low morale is the most cited reason for leaving.

Which is the appropriate question to ask at this stage?

Options:

1. Why is morale so low in our company?

2. Why are we losing employees to this competitor in particular? 3. How can we improve morale here?

4. Why are employees citing low morale as a factor?

Answer

Option 1: This is the correct option. If low morale is the most cited reason, you need to focus on this information and probe to find out more.

Option 2: This is an incorrect option. Asking this question shifts the focus away from the problem at hand. Instead of focusing on a competitor, address the morale issue in your company.

Option 3: This is an incorrect option. This question skips a layer of questioning. You need to know why morale is low before you can do

64. Problem-Solving and Decision-Making Strategies
something about it.

Option 4: This is an incorrect option. You can't observe why employees are citing low morale.

Question

Employees say they lack advancement opportunities and don't have designated career paths.

How do you respond to this stage of the five-why analysis?

Options:

1. Ask "Why don't we have career paths mapped out for each job role?"

2. Ask "Why are career paths important to employees?"

3. Ask "Why should we use resources to map out career paths?"

4. Recognize that not having career paths mapped out is the root cause of the problem.

Answer

Option 1: This is the correct option. This question is a logical response to the statement and digs deeper to the next causal layer.

Option 2: This is an incorrect option. This question asks about factors that aren't observable. Trying to find this out will be a waste of time and energy.

Option 3: This is an incorrect option. This question isn't focused on the statement at hand. Asking why your company doesn't have career paths mapped out would be more illuminating.

Option 4: This is an incorrect option. To address this root cause, you still need to know why career paths aren't mapped out in the first place. This shows there's another causal layer to this problem.

Question

Your team finds out that the Human Resource Department began mapping out career paths for various jobs but had to halt the project because it was understaffed and under-resourced.

How do you respond to this stage of the five-why analysis?

Options:

1. Recognize that HR's understaffing is the root cause of the problem.

2. Ask "Why is HR understaffed?"

3. Ask "What issues are members of the HR Department devoting time and resources to?"

4. Ask "Why did HR stop mapping out career paths?"

Answer

Option 1: This is the correct option. The fact that the HR Department is too understaffed to complete

64. Problem-Solving and Decision-Making Strategies

career development plans is the root cause of the problem. Your team can now work to address this issue.

Option 2: This is an incorrect option. The fact that HR is understaffed is clearly the root cause of the issue. Going further won't shed any more light on the problem.

Option 3: This is an incorrect option. This question is beside the point – the root cause of the problem at hand is that HR is understaffed, so this is the issue you should address to solve your problem.

Option 4: This is an incorrect option. Asking this addresses an earlier statement that's already been discussed.

Problem-solving Solutions: Looking Beyond the Obvious

To analyze a problem, you first collect as many potential solutions as possible. You then generate a shortlist of the most appropriate potential solutions. Next you analyze the shortlist.

To choose the most financially beneficial solution, you use a cost-benefit analysis. This technique follows eight steps. First you decide on a time scale for the analysis. You then brainstorm the costs and the benefits for each potential solution, and express them in monetary terms. You sum up the costs and the benefits, and then calculate the cost-benefit ratio for each solution by dividing the total benefits by the total costs. Finally, you compare the ratios and choose the solution with the best ratio.

Collecting potential solutions

Have you ever had a really bad toothache? It's unpleasant to say the least. Imagine you visit your local dental practice and the dentist has a quick look and then inserts some filler into a small cavity. Two days later you're still in agony and are back at the dental practice. An X-ray reveals that your nerve is infected. In this situation, the dentist assumed the problem was a cavity without analyzing further to uncover the root cause – the infected nerve.

To find a solution to a problem, you should analyze the problem until you find its root. Once you've done so, you can then explore different solutions.

At this stage in the process, you should try and generate as many potential solutions as possible. You should have a wide and varied range of solutions from different perspectives because this will help you come up with the most effective solution.

When you want to find a solution for a problem, it is important that you look beyond the obvious. There are several different ways to generate solutions:

- brainstorming in a group of people with experts and non-experts,

- doing additional research with primary and secondary sources,
- looking outside your own experience by consulting with others, and
- consulting the decision maker who will select the final solution.

Brainstorming

Brainstorming enables you to have a relaxed discussion about the solutions that individuals in a group propose. Having experts as well as non-experts in this group ensures the discussion will extract various perspectives.

Additional research

Additional research – including an analysis of documents of both primary and secondary origins – helps you add more solutions and feedback to your existing ideas.

Looking outside our own experience

It's helpful to take note of people's experiences when dealing with similar problems. You can interview them to find out what they did and if it was effective. You can also investigate benchmarks and best practices. However, it's important not to assume a solution will work for your problem just because it worked for someone else's.

Consulting the decision maker

64. Problem-Solving and Decision-Making Strategies

At the end of the day, the decision maker will select the final solution, so it's useful to ask for the decision maker's opinion. The decision maker will have the appropriate objectives in mind and will most likely be able to contribute some very good ideas.

Now that you have a general list of possible solutions, you can analyze them in more depth to decide which options are the most advantageous.

To shortlist the most advantageous solutions, it's useful to go back to the definition of the problem. You can then compare the objectives of solving the problem to those of the new possible solutions and delete the least appropriate. This provides you with a neat shortlist of your most appropriate potential solutions. Sometimes, you may need to make adjustments to the definition of the problem.

Shortlisting your solutions

The problem-solving model consists of six steps. Choosing the best solution is step four. After you've created your shortlist, you can analyze the potential solutions so that you're able to select the one that's most suitable.

You can choose between three techniques when analyzing the potential solutions in your shortlist: cost- benefit analysis, multi-attribute analysis, and force-field analysis.

Out of the three, cost-benefit analysis is a very popular way to analyze the different solutions because financial benefits are frequently the deciding factor. This type of analysis enables you to select the most financially beneficial solution.

To do a cost-benefit analysis, you complete eight steps:

1. determine a time scale for your analysis,
2. brainstorm a list of cost factors associated with implementing the potential solution,
3. specify the costs in monetary terms,
4. brainstorm a list of benefits that your potential solution will have,
5. translate the benefits into monetary or tangible terms for your solution,
6. sum the total costs and benefits,

64. Problem-Solving and Decision-Making Strategies

7. determine the cost-benefit ratio of your solution, and

8. choose the best solution that gives the best return.

1. Determine time scale
You first have to determine a time scale for your analysis. For example, you might predict the prospective costs and benefits over a five-year time scale.

2. Brainstorm list of cost factors
You need to brainstorm all the cost factors associated with implementing the potential solution. This might include new machinery, training, advertising, and overtime.

3. Specify costs
For each cost factor, you specify the cost in monetary terms.

4. Brainstorm list of benefits
Now you brainstorm a list of all the benefits that your potential solution will have. This might include benefits like increased sales, reduced overtime, and increased productivity.

5. Translate benefits into monetary terms
For each potential benefit of the solution, you need to translate it into an actual monetary value.

6. Sum up total costs and benefits

You sum all of the costs to get total costs and all the benefits to get total benefits.

7. Determine cost-benefit ratio

To determine the cost-benefit ratio, you divide the total benefits by the total costs. For example, if the total benefit was $1,500 and the total cost was $1,000, the ratio is 1:1.5. This means that for every one part cost, there is 1.5 part benefit. In this case, the company benefits from the solution.

In another example, a solution has a total benefit of $500 and a total cost of $1,000. The ratio is 1:0.5, which means that for every one part cost there is only a 0.5 part benefit, which works out to be a loss.

8. Choose best solution

Finally, you compare all the solutions with their cost-benefit analysis and ratios, and choose the most effective solution for your problem. If the ratios are too close to decide, you can compare the net benefit in monetary terms.

Cost-benefit analysis

Say a coffee outlet is experiencing problems serving its customers. Customers are complaining that it takes too long for them to get their orders. The root of the problem is that customer demand has increased. The shop owners brainstorm possible solutions and come up with a shortlist of two.

These are the two potential solutions:
- hiring two new employees, or
- increasing the equipment by buying three self-service coffee machines.

The owners decide to do a cost-benefit analysis to determine which solution will be the most economical. The first step is to determine a time scale for the analysis. They decide to research costs and benefits on a monthly basis.

After deciding on a time scale, the team then brainstorms costs and benefits for each potential solution.

Employing two new staff

Hiring new employees will increase wage costs, and new employees will obviously need training. However, having two extra employees will also lead to increased productivity and sales.

Buying three self-service coffee machines

Buying self-service coffee machines will result in monthly capital costs and initial set-up costs. The benefits are the same as for hiring new employees – increased productivity and sales.

The team enters the costs and benefits for each potential solution into a table to make them easier to analyze. The team then works out the monetary values for each cost and each benefit and enters the values in the table.

Now team members begin to analyze the first solution – hiring two new employees. To get the total costs, team members add all the costs together, resulting in a total of $8,000. They then add the benefits, coming up with a total of $13,000.

Then, to calculate the cost-benefit ratio, the team divides the total benefits by the total costs. This results in a ratio of 1:1.63. The team calculates the solution's net benefit by subtracting total costs from total benefits. The result is a net benefit of $5,000.

The store owners repeat the analysis for the other potential solution. The cost-benefit ratio of buying self-service coffee machines is 1:2.5, which is better than the ratio of 1:1.63 for the first solution, hiring two new employees. Also, the net profit of buying self-service machines, $6,000, is larger than the other potential solution's net profit of $5,000.

64. Problem-Solving and Decision-Making Strategies

Therefore, the most efficient solution is buying three new self-service coffee machines.

Case Study: Question 1 of 3
Scenario

A manufacturing company needs to increase output to meet its growing market. Three possible solutions are being considered, including a new conveyor belt, introducing 24/7 production and shift work, and outsourcing the production of additional demand to a partner.

Answer the questions about the manufacturing company and the cost-benefit analysis of its potential solutions in the given order.

Question

You have already completed a cost-benefit analysis for 24/7 shift work and outsourcing.

If you choose to introduce a new conveyor belt, the monthly pro-rated capital will cost $13,500, and the installation and maintenance cost will be $3,500 per month. The new conveyor belt will help increase productivity by $30,000 per month and also reduce employee costs by $7,000 per month. However, employees will need to be trained, which will cost $4,500. Also, the setup downtime of the conveyor belt will be $1,500. If you choose to implement the conveyor belt solution, the company will realize a quality cost savings of $5,000 per month.

What are monetary values of the individual benefits of installing a conveyor belt?

Options:

1. $3,500
2. $4,500
3. $1,500
4. $30,000
5. $7,000
6. $5,000

Answer

Option 1: This option is incorrect. Installing the conveyor belt will be a cost to the company. Option 2: This option is incorrect. It will cost the company $4,500 to train employees. This isn't a benefit.

Option 3: This is an incorrect option. Setting up the conveyor belt will take time and will have a negative effect on production. Having the conveyor belt offline will cost the company $1,500 as production will not be halted.

Option 4: This option is correct. Increased productivity will benefit the company. The new productivity is equal to $30,000.

Option 5: This is a correct option. Reduced employee costs will save the company $7,000, which is a benefit.

Option 6: This option is correct. Installing a new

64. Problem-Solving and Decision-Making Strategies conveyor belt will save the company $5,000 on quality-related issues. This is a benefit for the company.

Case Study: Question 2 of 3

To complete the cost-benefit analysis of the potential solution, you need to do some calculations.

Match the types of figure to the correct values. Not all values will receive a match.

Options:
A. Total costs
B. Total benefits
C. Cost-benefit ratio
D. Net benefit

Targets:
1. $23,000
2. $42,000
3. 1:1.83
4. $19,000
5. $65,000
6. 1:0.55

Answer

To get the total costs, you add all the costs together. In this case, you add $13,500, $3,500, $4,500, and $1,500, which equals $23,000.

To get the total benefits, you add all the benefits together. In this case, you add $30,000, $7,000, and

$5,000, resulting in a total of $42,000.

To get the cost-benefit ratio, you divide the total benefits by the total costs. So you divide $42,000 by $23,000, which equals 1.83. So the cost-benefit ratio is 1 to 1.83.

To calculate the net benefit, you subtract the total costs from the total benefits. In this case, you subtract $23,000 from $42,000, resulting in a net benefit of $19,000.

To determine the net benefit, you subtract the total costs from the total benefits; you don't add the total costs and the total benefits together.

To arrive at a ratio of 1:0.55, you would've had to divide the total costs by the total benefits. You actually divide the total benefits by the total costs to calculate the cost-benefit ratio.

Case Study: Question 3 of 3

From the completed cost-benefit analysis, you can assess which solution makes most financial sense.

Which potential solution should the company implement?

Options:
1. New conveyor belt
2. 24/7 production and shift work
3. Outsource

64. Problem-Solving and Decision-Making Strategies

Answer

Option 1: This is the correct option. The net benefit of installing a new conveyor belt is much higher than the net benefit of the other two potential solutions. Also, the cost-benefit ratio for this solution is better than that of the other solutions.

Option 2: This option is incorrect. Out of the three options, the conveyor belt solution has the highest net benefit and the best cost-benefit ratio. Therefore, the company should implement that solution.

Option 3: This option is incorrect. The conveyor belt solution has the highest net benefit and the best cost-benefit ratio out of all the proposed solutions. The company should therefore implement that solution.

Decision Making: The Fundamentals
The Basics of Effective Decision Making
Decision-making Styles
Adapting Your Decision-making Style

The Basics of Effective Decision Making

Decision making is more than simply making a choice – it involves analyzing potential decisions while focusing on a desired outcome. Effective decision making is essential for personal and professional success, is a necessary skill for career advancement, leads to greater efficiency, moves organizations forward and allows for greater confidence in decisions.

Consciously following the steps in a clear process can result in more effective decisions. The five steps in a basic decision-making model are establishing a context for success, framing the issue properly, generating alternatives, evaluating the alternatives, and choosing the best alternative.

Effective decision making

Sometimes decisions are so small you don't even make them consciously. Others require careful thought and deliberation. You make thousands of decisions every day, in your personal and professional life. Just a few examples are what to have for breakfast, the best way to get to the office, how to meet your sales targets, whether to ask for a raise, and whether your company should merge with another company.

So what is involved in decision making? Most people think of it as the simple act of making a choice.

But decision making is more than this. It's a process that involves identifying alternatives, analyzing them in terms of their consequences and the outcome you want, and choosing the alternative you think is best.

People make decisions for a lot of different reasons, both good and bad. For example, your motive in making a decision may be to solve a particular problem or move an organization forward. Or it may be to gloss over a mistake, improve your standing in an organization or fit into a new peer group.

64. Problem-Solving and Decision-Making Strategies

Solve a problem

Decisions are often needed to solve problems. If a number of alternative remedies are available, you have to choose the best one.

For example, if you're constantly missing your work deadlines despite your best efforts, you might make a decision to talk to your boss about reducing your workload or to develop a better system for managing your time.

Move an organization forward

You may need to decide how to reach a particular work-related goal or how to take advantage of a situation to move your organization forward. Often these decisions are complex and difficult, so it's important you have effective decision-making skills.

For example, you might need to decide how to gain the upper hand over a competitor, or whether a different pricing strategy would improve profitability.

Gloss over a mistake

Sometimes people make decisions in order to avoid drawing attention to mistakes they made in the past. This can have negative consequences because the decisions aren't made for the good of other people or an organization.

For example, reluctance to share information

about previous unsuccessful initiatives increases the chances that others will repeat the same mistakes.

Improve your standing

A desire to improve your standing, gain prestige, or impress others are not good reasons to make a decision.

For example, a manager who implements a new process just to appear efficient or busy – rather than because the process will improve productivity – is doing so for personal gain rather than the good of an organization.

Fit into a new peer group

Sometimes people make decisions because they think these will help them fit in or make friends.

For example, a new manager may decide to grant all employees' requests. This manager may be popular initially, but is unlikely to gain credibility or respect in the long run.

Given the amount and variety of decisions people make every day, it's important to be good at decision making.

First it's important for your personal and professional success. People who don't think things through or who consistently make rash or bad decisions struggle to achieve their goals and find fulfillment.

64. Problem-Solving and Decision-Making Strategies

Good decision making is also necessary for career advancement. Any position of authority or responsibility requires good decison-making abilities. For example, managers are typically required to be decisive and able to choose the right course of action in a crisis. Alternatively, they need to know when it's appropriate to involve others in the decision-making process.

It's possible to waste a lot of effort and money by pursuing the wrong course of action and then having to fix mistakes. Procrastinating can also waste valuable time. As an effective decision maker, you'll make more efficient use of your time and resources. Remember, however, that good decision makers make timely decisions – this should not be mistaken for rash or impulsive decisions.

Good decisions move teams and organizations forward and help them achieve their goals. For example, a company benefits if it makes good, quick decisions ahead of its competitors.

Finally, as an effective decision maker, you'll be more confident about the outcome of your decisions. This is because you will have carefully analyzed the potential consequences of your actions.

If you're offered a new job, for example, you'd want to carefully consider the pros and cons of accepting it. That way, you'd be happier with your decision and wouldn't come to regret it later.

Question

Why is effective decision making important?

Options:

1. It's important for achieving personal success
2. It's necessary for professional advancement
3. It can prevent wasted time, effort, and money
4. It can give organizations a competitive edge
5. It can improve your confidence in the choices you make
6. It ensures you can be quick in reaching firm decisions
7. It prevents you from having to rely on the participation of others in reaching decisions

Answer

Option 1: This option is correct. If you're an effective decision maker, you'll find it easier to succeed personally and professionally because it will be easier to achieve your goals.

Option 2: This is a correct option. Positions with more responsibility or authority require good decision- making skills, so having these skills is necessary for advancing your career.

Option 3: This option is correct. By making good decisions, you make better use of your time and resources. This is because effective decisions

64. Problem-Solving and Decision-Making Strategies prevent mistakes and the need to redo work. Effective decision making can also prevent you from procrastinating, which wastes time and money.

Option 4: This option is correct. Effective decision making allows organizations to move forward and helps them achieve their goals.

Option 5: This option is correct. Good decision making involves thinking through the consequences of the various alternatives or courses of actions that are available. Doing this helps ensure you can be confident about the outcomes of decisions you make.

Option 6: This is an incorrect option. Effective decision making isn't necessarily faster. It involves careful evaluation of alternatives, rather than jumping to rash, quick decisions.

Option 7: This option is incorrect. Effective decision making doesn't necessarily involve making all decisions independently. It may be important to consult others or to ensure that everyone in a group reaches consensus before a final decision is made.

The decision-making process

You follow certain logical steps when you make a decision, even if you don't do this consciously.

However, it's useful to think of decision making as a conscious and established process so that you don't miss or compromise any of the steps. Doing this increases your chances of making effective decisions.

A basic decision-making model includes five steps. First you establish a context for success. Then you frame the issue properly. You generate alternatives, evaluate the alternatives, and, finally, you choose the best alternative.

Consider how the model can be applied in practice. Catherine is a departmental head for a nationwide company that commissions and distributes college-level textbooks. A recent drop in sales and profitability means her team has to decide on the best strategies and corrective measures to ensure sales and profit growth.

The first step is to establish a context in which the problem can be effectively addressed. To do this, you involve the right people, keep the decision group small, encourage their participation, choose diverse settings for meetings, and avoid advocacy.

64. Problem-Solving and Decision-Making Strategies

Involve the right people

You should involve a combination of knowledgeable people with divergent opinions – both opponents and supporters of the idea being debated. You also need someone in a position of authority who can delegate tasks and resources.

For example, Catherine's team should include someone from the Finance and Accounting Department who knows sales and profitability trends for each product line. She should also invite zonal managers to the team that will be implementing the chosen course of action.

Keep the decision group small

Although you shouldn't leave out anyone with valuable expertise, you should keep the decision group to a manageable size. Including too large a group is likely to slow down the decision- making process. It may also intimidate those who have valid ideas but aren't used to speaking in a crowd.

Catherine is careful in identifying who should participate in the decision-making process. She identifies a group of six people, each of whom has skills or knowledge relevant to the problem that must be addressed.

Encourage participation

You encourage participation by demonstrating you value minority views and different opinions. By ensuring people won't be afraid to air their worries or criticisms, you facilitate healthy debate.

Catherine makes sure that everyone at the meeting gets a say.

Choose diverse settings

People are more creative and more likely to voice their opinions freely when they are in new settings.

So although Catherine usually leads discussions at the head of the boardroom table, she decides to rearrange the furniture into a circle to diffuse the power dynamics that usually apply.

Avoid advocacy

Although it's important to make room for different opinions, everyone in the group should present balanced arguments for a position and be open to constructive criticism.

Catherine knows that Mark generally plays the devil's advocate; she encourages him to consider the other side too, and to present a balanced argument. She also makes a positive environment for everyone in the team to offer and welcome constructive criticism.

Once you've established a context for success, the next step is to frame the issue properly.

Your experiences and expectations affect your

64. Problem-Solving and Decision-Making Strategies

perceptions. So when a complicated situation arises, you need to frame it properly to make sure you address the real issue.

Catherine asks her team members what they think about the situation. Whereas Catherine believes their advertising strategy is outdated, Richard thinks the books' authors don't have the required level of expertise. Catherine and Richard's different frames would generate divergent solutions if they were acting alone.

To avoid misframing, don't simply accept your initial perceptions. Instead, try to pinpoint your biases and those of other people. Seek out the perspectives of others in the decision-making team, and try to approach the issue from several angles.

Catherine gains some valuable information by not imposing her own framing of the situation on others. If she'd started the meeting by saying "We need to think of ways to improve our advertising strategy," the team's focus would have been very different.

It's good to be creative at this stage of the decision-making process – try to come up with as many ways of understanding the situation as you can.

Catherine's team even tries to interpret the issue from an outsider's perspective. Everyone asks themselves what they'd think of the textbooks if they were using them at college. How do the textbooks compare to others in terms of value for money? Is it easy for lecturers to find out what books are on offer?

Once you have a thorough understanding of the issue, you need to generate alternatives. Often more options are open to you than you originally think. You find them by brainstorming and involving creative people in the decision-making team.

Brainstorm

You brainstorm by writing down as many possible alternatives as you can, without criticizing or judging the ideas. It's more effective to do this as a team because everyone brings fresh ideas to the table.

In Catherine's case, she tries to get everyone to contribute. As Lucy is a shy person, Catherine asks everyone to write down their ideas and pass them to her so she can list them on a whiteboard. This ensures that everyone contributes.

Involve creative people

When you form a decision-making team, you should include people who tackle problems energetically and are likely to have valuable insights and original ideas. A diverse group of people is less

64. Problem-Solving and Decision-Making Strategies

likely to agree immediately and this will spark healthy debate.

To counteract the friction this inevitably causes, Catherine lays down some ground rules – everyone has to listen properly to the others and show respect for their opinions. Everyone is encouraged to challenge ideas they don't agree with – but not to make any personal attacks.

When generating alternatives, it's important to come up with strong, viable choices. A good alternative has these characteristics:
- be unique and broadly constructed so it isn't just a variation of another idea,
- take the organization's resources and constraints into account, and
- offer a real choice that hasn't just been included to make up the numbers or make another idea seem better than it really is.

Through brainstorming and the efforts of the whole team, Catherine's team has come up with a number of ways to counteract the recent drop in sales. They include developing new lines; attracting new, cutting-edge authors; enticing best-selling authors from other publishing companies; optimizing book quality to decrease costs; and investing in a new marketing campaign.

Your list should include as many alternatives as possible, but it shouldn't become overwhelming. Then you need to evaluate these alternatives. This involves determining how well each alternative meets your objective.

Often, as in Catherine's case, the financial implications will be the deciding factor. Her team has to decide on the option that will increase sales and profitability most.

You can use a number of tools to help you evaluate possible alternatives. These include the prioritization matrix, the trade-off table, the decision tree, and various software programs.

Prioritization matrix

Successfully evaluating alternative solutions might require you to weigh them against criteria specific to a problem. You can do this numerically. Using a prioritization matrix, you detail and give each of the problem's criteria a numeric value reflecting its priority.

You then address your alternative solutions. Assess how well they meet the needs of individual criteria. Then give them a numeric rating – say on a scale of one to ten – in rows beneath the relevant criteria.

You then total the product set of each alternative

64. Problem-Solving and Decision-Making Strategies

matched to each criterion's priority rating. In other words, you multiply the values of each criterion and its matching alternative. You then add together the total for each alternative. The alternative with the highest total is that which is best suited to meeting your objective.

In this example of a prioritization matrix the column headers are Increase profits, Improve product quality, Implement quickly, and Score. The row headers list two alternatives: A and B.

For alternative A, the calculation for "Increase profits" is 4 multiplied by 5 equals 20, for "Improve product quality" it's 3 multiplied by 9 equals 27, and for "Implement quickly" it's 1 multiplied by 9 equals 9. The score for alternative A is the sum of 20, 27, and 9, which is 56.

For alternative B, the calculation for "Increase profits" is 4 multiplied by 6 equals 24, for "Improve product quality" it's 3 multiplied by 2 equals 6, and for "Implement quickly" it's 1 multiplied by 2 equals 2. The score for alternative B is the sum of 24, 6, and 2, which is 32.

Trade-off table

In a trade-off table, like in a prioritization matrix, you compare how well each alternative meets your objectives. You list the objectives, fill in specific data about the alternatives, and weigh them against each other. In this example, option B's bigger profits are offset by low product quality and slow implementation.

In this example of a trade-off table, two alternatives are presented: alternative A and alternative B. The profitability for alternative A is $50,000, and for alternative B, it's $60,000. For alternative A, the product quality will show great improvement, while alternative B will only show slight improvement. The implementation for alternative A can begin in one month, while alternative B can begin in six months.

Decision tree

A decision tree is a graphic representation of each alternative's possible outcomes. Outcomes can include success and failure percentage estimates, profitability, and other possible events. The complexity of the diagram depends on the complexity of the problem. Although it won't tell you which alternative to choose, it can help your team assess and compare the possible outcomes of the alternatives.

A problem has two possible solutions arrayed beneath it – Option A and Option B. At a lower level, and stemming from each option, are two courses of action – to abandon or continue implementation. The tree shows us that, in Option

B's case, its continuance would result in a 65 percent chance of success and a 35 percent chance of failure, while its abandonment would decrease its chances of success to 55 percent and increase its possibility of failure to 45 percent.

Software programs

Various software programs can assist you when evaluating alternatives requires sifting through lots of data. These range from simple spreadsheets you use to add up figures to more sophisticated programs tailor-made for individual companies.

Catherine's team members use a prioritization matrix to evaluate the alternative solutions. They consider each solution under a range of different weighted criteria such as cost, ease of implementation, time, and stakeholder impact. After summing the scores, the team discovers that developing new lines, attracting new, cutting-edge authors, and investing in a new marketing campaign are the top three potential solutions.

Once you've considered the merits of each alternative, you need to choose the best alternative. An important aspect of this is that you need to know when to end the deliberations.

If you're too quick to make a decision, you might miss a better alternative or fail to think through the pitfalls of your choice. But if you take too long, you might miss valuable opportunities. Insisting on hearing out every idea and opinion can simply waste time and resources.

Choosing the best decision is not the end of the process – you'll have to turn the decision into action. First you need to communicate your team's finding to everyone who was and will be involved. Show consideration to the people who have given their input by saying why their suggestions were or were not taken up.

To implement your decision, you'll probably need to delegate, set deadlines, and follow up. Make sure everyone is aware of their responsibilities and of how they may be affected.

Because her team can't decide on the best alternative, Catherine takes responsibility for making the final decision. She decides that introducing new lines is the best way to increase sales and profitability. She lends credibility to her decision by letting everyone know why she discarded some suggestions, and reiterates that everyone's input contributed to the final decision. As a result, her team thinks the process was effective and fair.

Catherine delegates tasks by asking Richard to notify the Marketing, Commissioning, Production,

64. Problem-Solving and Decision-Making Strategies

and other affected departments by the end of the day. Then she asks three team members to produce a schedule for the implementation of the decision, and she follows up to make sure everything is going smoothly.

Question

Ahmed is the features editor for an adventure travel magazine. He has been getting complaints that feature articles in the magazine are too tired and contrived. Now he wants to decide on a feature for the next issue.

Sequence the example of the steps in the decision-making model.

Options:

A. He asks a few key people and some very creative people to attend a planning session

B. He asks for ways to improve his department's feature articles

C. The team brainstorms, thinking of unique and viable feature articles

D. The team uses a prioritization matrix to evaluate solutions under a range of criteria

E. He explains why the chosen article is the best alternative and promises to pass on all reader feedback he receives

Answer

He asks a few key people and some very creative people to attend a planning session is ranked the first step.

The first step is to establish a context for success. One way that Ahmed does this is by ensuring the right people participate in the decision-making process. This includes people with authority, as well as people who will have some creative ideas.

He asks for ways to improve his department's feature articles is ranked the second step.

The second step, after establishing a context for success – in this case, low- budget adventure vacations, is to frame the issue properly. Ahmed does this by

getting everyone's input on the problem in case he has misunderstood it.

The team brainstorms, thinking of unique and viable feature articles is ranked the third step.

The third step is to generate alternatives, each of which should be unique and feasible. Ahmed's team does this by brainstorming.

The team uses a prioritization matrix to evaluate solutions under a range of criteria is ranked the fourth step.

The fourth step is to evaluate the alternatives. An example of a tool that can be used in this step is a

64. Problem-Solving and Decision-Making Strategies prioritization matrix, in which alternatives are scored and ranked based on how well they meet each of a set of criteria.

He explains why the chosen article is the best alternative and promises to pass on all reader feedback he receives is ranked the fifth step.

The fifth step is to choose the best alternative. In this case, Ahmed makes his selection final and closes the meeting. He ensures that everyone knows why the decision was made and keeps everyone in the loop.

Decision-making Styles

Approaches to the decision-making process can be categorized into four main styles – the authority or expert style, the consultative style, the traditional majority or voting style, and the consensus style. Each style has advantages and disadvantages, and suits specific situations.

The four decision-making styles

The project manager has to leave the office to deal with a family emergency. In her absence, Lisa and Anton are in charge of assembling a team to deal with the company's biggest sales pitch to date. Lisa feels she has a pretty good idea of everyone's strengths and weaknesses, so she has already decided on a team. Anton, on the other hand, wants to meet with senior staff members to discuss roles and responsibilities, and to make a collective decision on who'll be on the team.

Like in the case of Lisa and Anton, people may approach decisions in a variety of different ways.

Approaches to decision making can be categorized into four styles – the authority or expert style, the consultative style, the traditional majority or voting style, and the consensus style. Each style has unique characteristics.

Authority or expert style

The authority or expert style is traditionally used most in a business environment. You can think of it as the "I decide" style.

For example, a manager simply makes a decision and expects all staff to abide by it. Or a specialist makes an independent decision because others lack the expert knowledge on which the decision must be based.

Consultative style

The consultative style involves incorporating input from others in the decision you ultimately make. It can be likened to an "I decide but with your input" approach.

For instance, an executive gathers opinions from all floor managers before deciding how best to change a company's product-assembly process. The executive considers the floor managers' information, but retains responsibility for making the final decision.

Majority or voting style

The traditional majority or voting style is an approach in which the most popular decision is the one taken. This style is used quite often – sometimes just to get an idea of peoples' feelings on a particular matter. It's a process that can be quick and is good for coming to a decision that's based on what the majority of participants feel.

Consensus style

The consensus style of decision-making is a "we all decide" approach. It involves including all affected parties in the decision-making process and adopting a final decision only when everyone agrees that it's the best one.

64. Problem-Solving and Decision-Making Strategies

The consensus style incorporates the different opinions and perspectives of all individuals. The aim is to reach decisions everyone is happy with, although this can be time consuming.

Think about how you typically approach decisions. Which style do you most often use?

Remember that no one decision-making style is always best. The most appropriate style often depends on the situation you're facing.

In a crisis that requires an immediate response, for example, it can make the most sense for one person to make a decision and impose it on others – because this will be the fastest.

In another case, it may be vital to consider everyone's opinions and ask for their input so that a final decision is perceived as fair.

The four styles of decision making are sometimes grouped more simply into two broader categories. These are the authoritative style and the democratic style. The authoritative style is similar to the authority or expert style. The remaining three styles – consultative, traditional majority or voting, and consensus – are more democratic.

Take Rick for example. As a Human Resources manager, he reviews different medical aid plans for the insurance company he works for. He is careful to investigate the relative advantages and disadvantages of each plan. He then decides on one plan and informs employees about his decision.

Question

Which decision-making style did Rick use?

Options:

1. Authority or expert style
2. Consultative style
3. Traditional majority or voting style
4. Consensus style

Answer

Option 1: This is the correct option. Rick has used the authority or expert style – he relied on his own expertise to decide on a medical aid plan. He didn't consult staff members, but instead made a decision and then informed them about it.

Option 2: This option is incorrect. Rick didn't consult others as part of the decision-making process.

Option 3: This is an incorrect option. Rick reached a decision independently, rather than asking the group and then going with whichever medical plan proved most popular.

Option 4: This option is incorrect. Rick reached a decision on his own, rather than asking the group and working to obtain everyone's agreement on

64. Problem-Solving and Decision-Making Strategies

which was the best plan.

Rick uses the authority or expert style because it enables him to reach a decision quickly. However, some employees feel their needs haven't been taken into account. For example, employees with families favor a plan with extra coverage for visits to pediatricians. Others prefer a more basic plan with lower premiums.

If you use the authority or expert style of decision making, you should discuss the decision you make with those who are affected by it. You should explain why you reached the decision and what effects it'll have on employees and your organization as a whole.

If you don't approach this style properly, you could create a situation in which employees feel alienated and unappreciated – they may feel that their opinions or ideas don't count, or that your approach is unfair.

Although an advantage of the authority or expert style is that a decision can be made quite quickly, a disadvantage is that other individuals aren't involved. They don't have a say and aren't called on to develop their decision-making skills.

Also, with this style, the quality of the decision that's made depends solely on the knowledge and expertise of one person.

If Rick uses the consultative style of decision making to choose a medical aid plan, he'll get valuable input from employees. However, he'll have to make it clear that he's responsible for the final decision. Also, it's important that he actually wants and values input from others. It only creates ill feeling if he consults others just to appease them and then doesn't appear to take their opinions into account.

The consultative approach to decision making takes longer than the authority or expert style but generally results in better, more informed decisions being made.

It also leads to a greater sense of trust because others feel that they've been part of the decision-making process.

Next, consider Gail, who's a manager at a clothing manufacturing company. The company is currently considering a proposed merger with a multinational textiles manufacturer. Gail organizes a meeting in which shareholders are asked to use private ballots to indicate whether or not they're in favor of the merger. She'll then tally up the results to determine a final decision.

Question

64. Problem-Solving and Decision-Making Strategies

Which decision-making style is Gail using?

Options:

1. Consensus style
2. Authority or expert style
3. Consultative style
4. Traditional majority or voting style

Answer

Gail is using the traditional majority or voting style. Shareholders vote and the decision that's most popular is the one that will be taken – even if a minority disagrees that it's the best one.

Although the traditional majority or voting style makes it possible to reach a decision quite quickly, it also has disadvantages.

This approach creates a "winners-and-losers" mentality. Unless the voting process is anonymous, people may vote with the majority – regardless of their actual views – so that they appear to support the "winning" or most popular decision.

It also means that those in the minority – the "losers" – don't get to air their views, although these may be valid ones nobody else has considered.

In a meeting with departmental employees about changing the office floor plan, Andrew decides to use the consensus style. He wants to change the floor plan to allow for more effective use of office space. He feels it's important to open the discussion up to all individuals who work in the office because it'll affect them directly. Also, by using the consensus style, he'll be able to gather different ideas about how best to utilize the office space.

The consensus style is often the most complicated and time consuming, but it's the best style to use if you really want all individuals concerned to be involved – so it's suitable in Andrew's situation.

Bear in mind though that because it's a time-consuming process, it's critical to ensure you use it only to decide on key issues.

If you choose this style but find that you're running out of time because it's taking too long, you can switch to a "back-up" style. After sufficient discussion, you may, for example, put the decision to a vote.

When you use the consensus style, it's not necessarily possible that everyone will reach complete agreement about the best decision. But once a decision is made, everyone involved must be able to answer yes to two important questions:

- "Am I able to live with the decision made?", and
- "Will I be able to support the decision that's made?"

64. Problem-Solving and Decision-Making Strategies

Live with the decision

For consensus to exist, everyone involved must feel able to accept a final decision – even if it isn't necessarily the one they'd reach independently.

So the decision that's chosen can't infringe on anyone's beliefs or ethics, or violate anyone's personal values.

Support the decision

Once a decision has been reached, those who participated should feel that they can support and uphold that decision when others question them about it, and through their attitudes and conduct. They should not leave the room feeling that they simply went along with a decision others made for them.

It's useful to be aware of the decision-making style you tend to favor but also to acknowledge the fact that some situations respond better to a different style of decision making.

Question

Match each scenario to the corresponding decision-making style.

Options:

A. Board members discuss alternative strategies

for downsizing, and adopt a strategy once it meets everyone's basic approval

B. A team leader decides on the criteria for determining staff bonuses and then explains these to the team

C. A manager asks staff to test different software and gets everyone's feedback before deciding which product to buy

D. At an annual general meeting, shareholders of a firm elect a new chairman of the board through a show of hands

Targets:

1. Consensus style
2. Authority or expert style
3. Consultative style
4. Traditional majority or voting style

Answer

Using the consensus style, the board members reach an agreement that they're all happy with. They can leave the meeting feeling able to live with and support the decision made.

The team leader uses the authority or expert style by deciding on criteria independently, rather than involving others in the decision-making process.

The manager is using a consultative approach by consulting others and taking their feedback into account, but retains the responsibility for making a

64. Problem-Solving and Decision-Making Strategies final decision.

The shareholders are using the traditional majority or voting style. They decide who the next chairperson of the board will be based on how the majority votes.

Adapting Your Decision-making Style

To be an effective decision maker, you have to tailor your decision-making style to each situation you face. While one style may work for a particular situation, it may not be appropriate in a different situation.

In each decision-making situation, you need to weigh up different factors, such as the time available, the importance of the decision, the availability of knowledge, the importance of securing buy-in from others, and experience. Once you've considered these elements, you should decide which decision-making style best suits the situation.

Influential factors in decision making

People make many different types of decisions, using a number of different decision-making styles. While one style may work for a particular situation, it may not be appropriate for another.

The most effective decision makers don't just stick to one decision-making style – they adapt their styles to suit the situations they face.

Several factors can influence your choice of style. These factors include the time that's available, the importance of a decision, required levels of knowledge, whether there's a need for buy-in from others, and your experience.

Time

If you need to make a decision quickly, it's generally most effective to use either the authority or expert style, or the traditional majority or voting style. These styles enable a decision to be reached rapidly.

For example, a team leader who has to decide between two alternatives may have a team vote and then simply go with the decision that's most popular. This is much less time consuming than consulting extensively with others or attempting to reach consensus in an open session with the team.

Importance

A decision may be especially important because it will have a significant impact or because it revolves around a controversial issue. In this case, it's best to use either the consultative style or the consensus style, provided time allows for this.

Before restructuring the departments in an organization, for example, a senior manager may consult various employees in the existing departments. This helps ensure the views of those who'll be affected are taken into account, and may improve perceptions that the final decision taken is a fair one.

Knowledge

If a team is very knowledgeable about an issue, it pays to use a consultative approach. This ensures everyone's expertise, insights, and experience can be pooled to determine the best possible decision.

However, if the team lacks knowledge about an issue, it's better to use the authority or expert style – and then to explain your decision and its likely impact.

For example, if everyone is familiar with relevant technologies, it's useful to involve the team in deciding on which technology is best for a particular purpose. If only you are familiar with the technologies, consulting others could just waste time.

Buy-in

When you need others to support a decision and its implementation, the majority or voting style may work. However, it's generally better to use the consensus style. That way, you know that you'll have the support of others going forward – and you're less likely to be undermined by parties who disagree with the decision.

For example, a manager is deciding whether to change his company's office productivity software set to a new, radically different set. Some employees are reluctant, so the manager discusses the matter with the group, and together, they reach consensus that he'll implement the new software, but provide ample training and time for everyone to adjust.

Experience

If your team has sufficient experience in making decisions as a group, you should use the consensus style. This style acknowledges your team members' capabilities and involves them in the decision-making process. However, if your team is inexperienced in group decision making, lacks relevant knowledge, or time is short, you should use a different style.

Say you need to identify the best of the available

technologies for a given purpose. It would be useful to use the consensus style with an experienced team that has relevant knowledge about the technologies. However, if this is likely to slow things down because team members typically struggle to collaborate, a different approach may be better.

Adapting your style

In each decision-making situation, you need to weigh up different factors and then decide which decision-making style best suits the situation. For example, how much time do you have to make the decision? How important is the decision? These and other issues are critical in choosing the style that will be the most effective.

People often need to make decisions in business contexts, and these may involve or affect teams or larger parts of an organization. Choosing the most appropriate decision-making style can have important consequences for you and the organization.

While it's often equally important to consider all the factors when you choose how best to approach a personal decision – or one you need to reach on your own – this topic focuses on decision making in a business environment.

An advertising agency manager is offered the opportunity to take on a promotions campaign for a company that specializes in mobile phone messaging. The manager is well acquainted with the relevant industry, but most members of his advertising team have very limited experience in the field. He's faced with the decision of whether to take the project or turn it down.

The manager is confident that his team can adapt to the new kind of work, and he knows that taking on the campaign could open the door to other lucrative opportunities. However, it could also involve a variety of risks.

The manager needs to make a decision quickly or he risks losing the project to a rival agency.

Question

Which decision-making style is most appropriate in this situation?

Options:

1. Consensus
2. Traditional majority or voting
3. Authority or expert
4. Consultative

Answer

Option 1: This option is incorrect. The consensus style would take too long, especially considering the team's lack of knowledge in the relevant field.

Option 2: This is an incorrect option. Putting the decision to a vote is not the best approach. Although it could result in a decision being reached quickly, team members in this case lack sufficient knowledge on which to base their own choices.

64. Problem-Solving and Decision-Making Strategies

Option 3: This is the correct option. The authority or expert style is best because it will enable the manager to make a decision quickly, while also taking into consideration the team's lack of knowledge in the relevant field.

Option 4: This is an incorrect option. The consultative approach would not be of much benefit because the team lacks knowledge about the relevant field.

Now consider a second example. A software development company relies on three streams of work, each handled by a separate team. Over the previous 12 months, the custom development team has been relatively inactive. The CEO now needs to decide whether to keep the team going, or to disband it and integrate its members into the company's other teams.

Keep?

Early indicators suggest that the company may secure a number of lucrative custom development projects in the coming year. If the team is disbanded, some very talented custom team members might opt to leave the company rather than move onto teams that handle different types of work.

Without these members, the company can't deliver the outstanding work that clients expect, and it may lose important custom development clients.

Disband?

The company is losing money by maintaining a relatively unproductive custom development team. If the team is disbanded and its members are reassigned, it's likely to increase the productivity of the remaining teams.

Additionally, having the team members work on new tasks could expand their professional abilities.

The managers of each of the three existing teams are very knowledgeable about their respective areas of work and know their team members well. It's important that these managers support whichever decision the CEO makes.

Question

Identify the two decision-making styles that are most appropriate for this situation.

Options:

1. Authority or expert
2. Consensus
3. Traditional majority or voting
4. Consultative

Answer

64. Problem-Solving and Decision-Making Strategies

Option 1: This option is incorrect. The authority or expert style is not appropriate because the CEO needs buy-in from the managers. Additionally, because the decision is so critical to the organization, the CEO should seek assistance from the managers, who have relevant knowledge.

Option 2: This option is correct. Because the decision is critical to the organization and it's important to secure the buy-in of managers, the CEO may choose to use the consensus style. This style is also appropriate because the need for a final decision isn't urgent. There should be enough time for everyone involved to reach consensus.

Option 3: This option is incorrect. The traditional majority or voting style is not likely to be effective with only four people – the CEO and three managers – participating in the vote. Also, the decision is an important one, making it wise to consider opinions and options rather than just voting on the alternatives.

Option 4: This option is correct. Because the decision is critical to the organization and the CEO has time, he could consult with the knowledgeable managers. This style is also advisable because it would help in securing buy-in from the managers, whose support the CEO requires.

In a third scenario, a successful law firm – comprising both experienced and newer lawyers – has grown to such an extent that it needs to move to bigger premises. The manager sets a deadline of one month to make a decision, and evaluates a number of potential office buildings – trying to find the best fit for the firm.

The decision is important because it'll affect all employees – especially with regard to traveling time to and from the new office.

The decision will also have an impact on client perceptions of the firm.

Question

Which decision-making styles are most appropriate in this situation?

Options:

1. Consultative
2. Authority or expert
3. Majority or voting
4. Consensus

Answer

Option 1: This is a correct option. Because the decision is so important and there's time available, it's appropriate for the manager to consult with staff. This style is also advisable because involving staff in the decision-making process will help ensure

64. Problem-Solving and Decision-Making Strategies

their support for the decision that's ultimately made, even if not all staff members agree.

Option 2: This is an incorrect option. The authority or expert style is not appropriate because the decision is too important, and will affect other stakeholders – whose opinions and knowledge should be taken into account. This style may be appropriate as a final resort if other approaches fail and time is running out – but it is not advisable as a first choice.

Option 3: This option is incorrect. Voting is not the best style in this situation because the decision is an important one and requires careful consideration. Also, individual staff members are likely to favor their own interests, without necessarily considering the best interests of the firm as a whole.

Option 4: This is a correct option. Because the decision is so important and time is available, the manager can try to get consensus from the staff. This will ensure that everyone supports the decision, or at the very least, is willing to live with it.

So next time you're faced with a decision, consider factors such as the time constraints, the experience and knowledge of those around you, the importance of the decision, and the level of buy-in required. Then use these factors to help you choose the decision-making style that is most appropriate.

Case Study: Question 1 of 3
Scenario

Julia owns a small but busy stationery shop. She employs a few permanent staff members – two drivers, two sales clerks, an administrative assistant, and a financial manager. Julie herself manages the business's relationships with suppliers.

Julia maintains a very strong grip, making almost all business-related decisions by herself. However, she now realizes that she needs to focus on adapting her decision-making style, depending on the situations she faces.

Answer the questions in any order to help Julia adapt her decision-making style based on the situations she faces.

Question

One of the company's delivery trucks has broken down, and an engine part needs to be replaced. There are three possible replacement parts, ranging in price and quality. The mechanic working on the truck needs to know which part to use, and he needs an answer within the next three days. Julia's drivers are motor vehicle enthusiasts, but Julia and the other employees don't know much about engines.

64. Problem-Solving and Decision-Making Strategies

Which decision styles are most appropriate for Julia to use?

Options:
1. Traditional majority or voting
2. Authority or expert
3. Consultative
4. Consensus

Answer

Option 1: This option is incorrect. The traditional majority or voting style is inappropriate because only two people – the drivers – have knowledge of the issue at hand.

Option 2: This is an incorrect option. The authority or expert style is inappropriate because Julia has very little knowledge of the relevant issue.

Option 3: This option is correct. Julia has a few days to make a decision, so there's time for her to consult the drivers – who have relevant knowledge.

Option 4: This option is correct. Julia has a few days to make a decision. Therefore, she can try to get consensus from the drivers, who have relevant knowledge.

Case Study: Question 2 of 3

During a telephone conversation, a supplier mentions that he's doubling the price of his stock. Julia realizes that if she's to retain the supplier, she'll make a loss on these items. Before Julia ends the conversation, she needs to decide whether to stay with the supplier or seek an alternative.

Which decision style is most appropriate in this case?

Options:

1. Consultative
2. Authority or expert
3. Consensus
4. Traditional majority or voting

Answer

Option 1: This is an incorrect option. Julia doesn't have time to consult with others, and she doesn't need to because supplier relations is her area of expertise.

Option 2: This is the correct option. Julia's the company's expert in the area of supplier relations, and she's under pressure to make a decision quickly.

Option 3: This is an incorrect option. Julia doesn't have time to get consensus, and she's the company's expert in the area of supplier relations. So it makes sense for her simply to make a final decision herself.

Option 4: This option is incorrect. Julia doesn't have time to organize a vote, and she's the company's expert in the area of supplier relations.

64. Problem-Solving and Decision-Making Strategies

Case Study: Question 3 of 3

At the end of a particularly stressful day, Julia decides to take her staff out for dinner. Unfortunately, most of the restaurants in the area are booked for the night, and she's left with a choice of only two places to eat. Julia and the staff are ready to go, so a quick decision is important.

Which decision style should Julia use to decide on a restaurant?

Options:

1. Consensus
2. Traditional majority or voting
3. Consultative
4. Authority or expert

Answer

Option 1: This is an incorrect option. Julia doesn't have enough time to get consensus from all the staff members.

Option 2: This is the correct option. A quick vote will give Julia an idea of which restaurant is the more popular choice among her staff members. Also, everyone involved is likely to recognize this as a fair way to settle on a decision.

Option 3: This option is incorrect. Julia doesn't have enough time to get each staff member's opinion.

Option 4: This is an incorrect option. Julia is no

more qualified to make the decision than her staff members – and putting the decision to a vote is one way to help ensure everyone's happy with the final decision.

Decision Making: Tools and Techniques
Dealing with Alternatives in Decision Making
Nominal Group Technique and Decision Making
Using ROI in Decision Making
Dealing with Alternatives in Decision Making

Dealing with Alternatives in Decision Making

A methodical decision-making process involves establishing a context for success, framing the issue properly, generating alternatives, evaluating the alternatives, and choosing the best alternative. Generating alternatives involves brainstorming ideas and ensuring proposed alternatives are broad, genuine, and feasible. Evaluating the alternatives involves analyzing their costs, benefits, risks, and relative feasibility.

You choose the best alternative by consolidating the results of evaluation, incorporating both subjective and objective information, and – in a group situation – reaching consensus or voting.

Generating alternatives

The decisions you make determine what you can accomplish, how you can accomplish it, and at what cost. But making a good decision isn't easy. Often there are many factors to take into account. This makes it important to use a methodical approach, which can help you to reach the best possible decisions.

A thorough decision-making model contains five steps. The first step involves ensuring you're in the right context. This may mean you ensure your team sets appropriate ground rules to encourage participation and deliberation, and you have the right people on a team to help you make a decision.

The second step requires you to properly frame the issue – that is you define, understand, and put it into context. If this isn't done, you're unlikely to make a suitable decision.

Steps three to five involve generating and evaluating alternatives, and finally selecting the best option from these alternatives. A variety of decision-making tools can assist you during these three steps. Several of these tools are covered in this course.

Question

Think about how you typically approach

problems or decisions.

How often do you choose to implement the first solution that comes to mind? **Options:**

1. Very often
2. Sometimes
3. Rarely

Answer

Option 1: Unfortunately, the first possible solution you generate isn't always the best one. Various tools and techniques can help you to identify other possible choices before making a decision. These tools accommodate your insights and gut feelings – which play important roles in decision making – and help you identify a broader range of options to choose from.

Option 2: The tools described in this course can be quickly applied in a variety of contexts to generate and evaluate potential solutions. The more solutions you're aware of, the more informed your final choice will be – and the more likely it is to be successful.

Option 3: If you rarely go with the first solution that comes to mind, it's likely that you make careful, informed decisions. However, various techniques and decision-making tools can help you determine further possible solutions to problems and enhance your capacity to evaluate them.

64. Problem-Solving and Decision-Making Strategies

If a single choice is presented without alternative options, the only possible decision is whether or not to proceed. The more alternatives you generate, the wider the choices you can make. So coming up with multiple solutions is an important step in any decision-making process.

You need several alternatives to make a good decision. However, generating too many alternatives makes it hard to grasp the situation or what is practical or possible in resolving it.

Also, you must assess and evaluate each alternative you generate. This takes time and energy, which you shouldn't squander by generating and assessing alternatives needlessly.

A useful way of generating alternatives is to brainstorm. In a brainstorming session, individuals or groups are encouraged to provide as many ideas as possible, without evaluating or judging them. This allows people to think creatively without self-censorship. The list is then thinned down to include only workable alternatives.

When brainstorming in a group situation, it may help if people generate ideas individually first. This can minimize censorship through peer pressure.

After brainstorming ideas, it's important to assess how good the alternatives are. Useful alternatives meet three minimum requirements – they're broad, genuine, and feasible.

Broad

When a range of alternatives is created, the goal is to cover all the major possible strategies and courses of action. So alternatives need to cover a fairly broad spectrum in order to lead to effective decisions.

If several potential courses of action are not covered by the alternatives, the alternatives may not give rise to adequate decisions. For example, a company wishing to augment its marketing strategy should generate alternatives that cover various media, including print, electronic, radio, and other marketing campaigns.

Genuine

Each alternative should represent a genuine option. It should not be suggested merely for the sake of making other potential decisions appear to be well thought out. You should also avoid rehashing ideas that have already been rejected.

Feasible

For an idea to be worth considering, it needs to be feasible – or realistic. If it can't be practically implemented, an alternative should not be considered. Alternatives that are clearly too costly,

64. Problem-Solving and Decision-Making Strategies

or require too many resources given the scope of the problem, should be scrapped.

To generate better alternatives, you take these steps:
- invite a creative and diverse group of people to participate in coming up with alternatives,
- consider existing solutions other companies have adopted,
- try to view the situation and possible solutions from multiple perspectives, and
- think creatively and consider whether alternatives can be combined.

Evaluating alternatives

Once alternatives have been generated, you need to evaluate them. This process involves assessing each alternative according to whether it meets your objectives in terms of costs, benefits, and feasibility. Key questions to consider are "What are the costs and benefits of each alternative?" and "Which alternative is most feasible?"

The costs and benefits of an alternative aren't always obvious, and can't always be quantified in financial terms. So you need to assess this aspect carefully, searching out hidden costs and benefits and considering a variety of angles and variables.

To assess the relative feasibility of each alternative, you ask whether the organization has adequate human resources, financial capacity, and infrastructure. Perhaps employees need to be trained or new people hired. You may need to overcome internal and external obstacles, including potential resistance from employees, and find workarounds to legal constraints.

Variables to consider when evaluating the feasibility of alternatives depend on the objectives you're pursuing. Commonly considered variables include financial impact, intangibles, time and other resources, risks, and ethics. During the evaluation

64. Problem-Solving and Decision-Making Strategies phase, you estimate how well each alternative meets the objectives you established at the outset of the process.

Financial impact

You assess financial impact in terms of costs and benefits. When assessing costs, you need to review the short-term and long-term expenses, hidden costs, potential savings, budgetary constraints, required financial liquidity or loans, and the likelihood of additional costs in the future.

When assessing benefits, you need to consider short- and long-term profits, the efficiency of income generation, and the likelihood of actually generating projected turnover. You also need to analyze whether each alternative will affect the net present value of the organization and when this effect is likely to be realized.

Intangibles

Costs and benefits may be significant yet intangible.

Intangibles to consider include an organization's reputation and image, customer satisfaction, employee morale, and the quality of products and services.

Time and other resources

The time it takes to implement an alternative is a

serious consideration because it has a direct impact on costs and on when you're likely to realize the benefits. You should take the probability of delays, as well as their potential impact and effects, into account.

You also need to consider resources such as employees, locations, buildings, and equipment for some alternatives.

Risks

You need to carefully assess the risks associated with an alternative. This includes determining the cost of the information you need to reduce uncertainties. You also need to assess each alternative's potential impact on profits, competitive advantage, competitors, suppliers, and customers.

Ethics

You need to consider the ethical implications of each alternative. Additionally, you need to ensure alternatives comply with the laws governing your organization.

The particular interests of customers, the community, and employees may each be affected differently. A useful benchmark is whether outsiders regard your organization's activities as ethical.

Choosing the best alternative

Once you've evaluated each of the alternatives separately, you should have a good understanding of them. Before you can choose the best alternative though, you need to compare your findings. Also, the members in a decision-making team may have different views of the costs, benefits, and feasibility of different alternatives, or they may have unaddressed subjective and qualitative concerns. For these reasons, you may fail to reach consensus on the best alternative.

Choosing the best alternative
To choose the best alternative, you need to consolidate your analyses and evaluations. This involves comparing and weighing the results for each alternative, integrating the results, generating consensus or voting, and making a decision.

For this you need rational methods for quantifying or standardizing assessments. For example, you may use financial measures to rank alternatives. You also need to ensure that subjective and qualitative considerations have been incorporated into these assessments.

To identify the best alternative, you need to

consolidate your analyses of all the alternatives and establish criteria. You then weigh and compare these criteria. In a group situation, you aim to generate consensus to ensure qualitative and subjective viewpoints are included. Voting techniques and financial criteria are also useful when you make a final decision.

Question

Match the activities and considerations to the decision-making steps with which they're associated. Each step may have more than one match.

Options:

A. Propose solutions that are broad, feasible, and genuine

B. Consider the ethical impacts and resource requirements of alternatives

C. Assess the probability of mishaps and their potential consequences

D. Achieve consensus among decision makers

E. Consolidate and compare analyses of the alternatives

F. Assemble an eclectic and creative team

Targets:

1. Step 3: Generate alternatives
2. Step 4: Evaluate alternatives

64. Problem-Solving and Decision-Making Strategies

3. Step 5: Choose the best alternative

Answer

Generating alternatives involves assembling a creative team and proposing a number of alternative solutions that are broad, feasible, and genuine.

Evaluating alternatives involves analyzing them by considering the variables that are relevant to the objectives of the decision. Variables may include ethical implications, resource requirements, and the degree of risk involved for each alternative.

To choose the best alternative, you need to consolidate and compare the results of evaluating all alternatives. In a group situation, you should also aim for consensus on the best decision, or use voting techniques.

Nominal Group Technique and Decision Making

The nominal group technique is a way of ensuring all members of a group contribute fully to the decision-making process, without being influenced by others' opinions.

Steps for implementing the nominal group technique include presenting the goal of the decision-making session, asking participants to generate alternatives individually, recording the alternatives, and then consolidating them as a group. Participants then rank a set of favored alternatives and the votes are tallied.

The six steps of NGT

Making decisions in group contexts can be tricky. Social dynamics can influence the decision-making process and it's difficult getting all the people in a group to volunteer their ideas. This stifles creativity and can lead to poor decisions. The nominal group technique is designed to avoid these pitfalls by ensuring all members of a group contribute fully to the decision-making process.

Provided it's rigorously and carefully applied, the nominal group technique – commonly abbreviated to NGT – helps a group to generate and prioritize alternatives, and to choose the best alternative by voting. So this technique is mostly used for steps three and five of the decision-making process.

The technique isn't used specifically to evaluate alternatives. It relies on individual members' judgments, rather than on formal, rigorous analysis or evaluation.

It's possible, however, to use the technique to arrive at a small set of favored alternatives, which the group then evaluates more thoroughly before reaching a final decision.

Sorin Dumitrascu

A group that participates in the nominal group technique is considered only "nominally" a group because the participants generate and vote on ideas privately, rather than by interacting as a group. This method works best with groups of eight to ten members.

When participants generate ideas anonymously and vote individually, it prevents them from being pressured or influenced by others.

As a result, it encourages creativity and diverse opinions.

The nominal group technique also encourages everyone in a group to participate fully in the decision- making process.

Using the nominal group technique involves six steps. First you present a group with one or more clear goals for decision making. Then you get the group members to generate alternatives. You record the alternatives where all members can access them, and then you consolidate them. Next you ask members to rank the alternatives. Finally, you tally the votes for each alternative to find the one the group has ranked as the best.

Step 1: Present goals

As the first step, you write the goals of the decision-making session on a whiteboard for the

64. Problem-Solving and Decision-Making Strategies

whole group to refer to. This helps ensure the session remains focused. You also ensure everyone understands the goals before moving to the next step.

Instead of a whiteboard, you could use a projector, a virtual medium, or any other means for displaying the goal and ensuring everyone can see it throughout the session.

Step 2: Generate alternatives

In the second step, each group member brainstorms alternative ideas for meeting the decision- making goals. Everyone does this separately and without discussing their ideas with others. This

helps ensure the opinions of others don't influence anyone else. Group members may record the alternatives they generate on index cards.

Step 3: Record the alternatives

Once the group members have generated alternatives, you gather the alternatives and record them in a place that everyone can see – on a whiteboard, for example.

Step 4: Consolidate the alternatives

Working together, the group consolidates similar alternatives to eliminate redundancy. You should explain any option that group members don't clearly understand, although it's important that no group member attempts to "sell" a particular alternative. The group moves on to the next step only once each alternative is clear to all participants.

Step 5: Rank the alternatives

Each person works alone to rank the alternatives. You ask group members to give their least preferable alternative a score of one and the highest score to the alternative they think is best. You can again use index cards for this step in the process.

Before beginning, it's important to decide how many alternatives to rank. If you rank too large a set of alternatives, the process of voting and tallying the results becomes unwieldy. Generally, it's best to limit members to ranking only their three to five preferred alternatives, giving their most preferred alternative the highest ranking.

Step 6: Tally votes

You tally the votes for each alternative in front of the group. You can then implement the idea with the most votes. Alternatively, you can use the results as a springboard for further discussion and evaluation of the favored choices.

Question

Put the steps of the nominal group technique in the correct order.

Options:

64. Problem-Solving and Decision-Making Strategies

A. Present goals

B. Generate alternatives C. Record the alternatives D. Consolidate alternatives E. Rank alternatives

F. Tally votes

Answer

Present goals is ranked the first step of the nominal group technique. Presenting the goals for the decision-making session is the first step in the process.

Generate alternatives is ranked the second step of the nominal group technique. Once everyone understands the goals of the session, each group member generates alternatives independently.

Record the alternatives is ranked the third step of the nominal group technique. As the third step, individually generated alternatives are gathered and written where all group members can access them.

Consolidate alternatives is ranked the fourth step of the nominal group technique. Consolidating the alternatives is the fourth step in the process. This means grouping similar alternatives together and eliminating redundancy.

Rank alternatives is ranked the fifth step of the nominal group technique. Once the alternatives have been consolidated, each member of the group ranks the alternatives independently.

Tally votes is ranked the sixth step of the nominal group technique. The final step in the process is to tally the results of the ranking process for each alternative. The alternative with the highest score is the one the group has decided is the best.

The nominal group technique improves on simple brainstorming in a number of ways:
- it ensures all members' participation is maximized, while preventing dominant individuals from influencing others,
- it encourages greater creativity,
- it generates more ideas, and
- it's more satisfying and inclusive for participants.

To be effective, a facilitator must properly manage the nominal group technique. For example, it's important that when people generate ideas or vote, they don't discuss what they're doing with others.

When clarifying and consolidating alternatives, participants shouldn't be drawn into a debate of the merits of the alternatives. Otherwise, persuasive individuals may sway the opinions of others, thereby distorting the results.

As a facilitator, you need to double-check that everybody understands the alternatives before

64. Problem-Solving and Decision-Making Strategies

finalizing the list. You also need to tally the results carefully, ensuring that all results are counted and totaled accurately. If there has been any significant confusion, the group should vote again.

Question

What are some of the good practices for facilitating a decision-making session using the nominal group technique?

Options:

1. Ensure group members generate ideas independently

2. Ensure everyone understands the goals before generating alternatives

3. Ensure participants give the highest scores to the alternatives they think are best

4. Ask participants to rank only their top three to five alternatives

5. Avoid modifying alternatives once you've written them on a whiteboard for everyone to see

6. Implement the alternative with the highest number of votes, without allowing further negotiation or discussion

Answer

Option 1: This option is correct. Each person should generate alternatives independently and anonymously to ensure some group members aren't influenced by others.

Option 2: This option is correct. You should record the goals of the session and ensure everyone understands them before group members begin generating alternatives. This helps to keep the session focused.

Option 3: This option is correct. If all participants give the highest scores to the alternatives they think are best, the alternative with the highest total score, once you've tallied the results, becomes the group's favorite option.

Option 4: This option is correct. To save time and make it easier to tally the votes, participants should limit themselves to ranking only their three to five most preferred alternatives.

Option 5: This option is incorrect. After the alternatives are written down for the group to consider, they should be consolidated. You should remove duplications and clarify the meaning of each alternative.

Option 6: This option is incorrect. Once the votes have been tallied, the group can still choose to discuss and analyze the preferred alternatives in more depth.

Using the six steps of NGT

Sally, the coordinator of a new outdoor organic market, has decided to use the nominal group technique to come up with ways to meet the goal of increasing sales. She sets up a workshop and invites the seven stallholders of the market to attend.

At the start of our workshop, I wrote the goal "To increase sales" on the whiteboard and asked participants if this goal was clear enough or if anyone had concerns about it.

After some discussion, we rewrote the goal as "Increasing the number of visitors to the market." This phrasing is clearer, because it excludes ideas for increasing sales that aren't related to the organic market.

Then I asked everyone to think of how we could achieve our goal. I had to remind some of the participants to work alone because, at this stage, I didn't want them to influence each other.

Step 3: Record the alternatives

"It was exciting to discover the ideas everyone came up with. I shuffled the index cards and got participants to read out one another's suggestions without knowing whose they were. This kept the process anonymous. Writing all the alternatives on the board was time consuming, but fun."

The alternatives the group generates for increasing visitors to the market are Hand out flyers, Billboard, Hot food stalls, Fires, Radio ads, Newspaper ads and articles, live music, Workshops, Create a mailing list, Repaint the entrance, Sunday lunches, A jungle gym, Raffles, Use media interviews to increase customer base, Create a web site, Play area for children, Pony rides, Hold sales, and Posters.

Step 4: Consolidate the alternatives

"Consolidating the alternatives was a quick process because most of them were easy to understand. For instance, we combined setting up a web site and creating an e-mailing list under a single alternative "Use online presence." At this point, almost all the alternatives seemed appealing and increasing the number of people who visit the market seemed like a huge job."

Once the alternatives are consolidated, they are: Paper media advertising, Warming offers (Fires and hot food), Entertainment (Live music, workshops), Children's entertainment (Pony rides, jungle gym), Repaint the entrance, Hold raffles and sales, Use online presence (Set up a web site, create an e-mailing list), Electronic advertising (Get interviewed by magazines, TV etc...)

Step 5: Rank the alternatives

"I asked participants to assign scores to their favorite four alternatives. They should give four points to the best idea and one point to the least useful idea of the four. We wrote our four choices on a fresh index card, and again, we shuffled them to keep the votes anonymous. I also used an index card to rank my top four alternatives."

Sally's rankings were: Children's entertainment – 4, Use online presence – 3, Entertainment – 2, and Repaint the entrance – 1.

Step 6: Tally votes

"I wrote all the votes on the board and tallied them. Once this was done, we took a short break and then had a long discussion about how to move forward.

We decided that the top three options – electronic advertising, paper media advertising, and setting up a children's entertainment area – were all priorities, and that the rest of the ideas could be shelved for now."

The alternative Warming offers gets a total of 2 votes. Entertainment gets 10 votes. Use online presence gets 9 votes. Hold raffles and sales gets 2 votes. Repaint the entrance gets 4 votes. Electronic advertising gets 21 votes. Paper media advertising gets 15 votes. Children's entertainment gets 17 votes.

The nominal group technique helped Sally's group identify good strategies for increasing traffic through the organic market. All the participants felt included in the decision-making process and a number of creative ideas were generated.

Case Study: Question 1 of 2
Scenario
You're leading a nominal group technique session with a small group of participants – the management team of a large industrial bakery.

The aim is to come up with the best way to reduce the cost of producing bread. The group of eight has already generated its alternatives and you have written them on a whiteboard.

Answer the questions in order.

Question
What will you do to lead the group into the next step?

Options:
1. Consolidate similar alternatives on the board, ensuring everyone understands each alternative

2. Hand out index cards and explain the ranking process to the group

3. Discuss the strengths and weaknesses of each

64. Problem-Solving and Decision-Making Strategies

alternative

4. Ask participants to individually rank their favorite alternatives

Answer

Option 1: This is the correct option. After you've written the alternatives on the whiteboard, the group should consolidate them to remove any duplication and clarify them, if necessary.

Option 2: This option is incorrect. Before you rank the alternatives, the group should consolidate them.

Option 3: This option is incorrect. Discussing the alternatives in this way leaves participants open to peer pressure. The group should consolidate them at this point and you should merely clarify the alternatives.

Option 4: This option is incorrect. First the group as a whole should consolidate the alternatives. Then participants should individually rank their favorite alternatives.

Case Study: Question 2 of 2

Now the group members have ranked their top choices. Seven of the members' rankings are written on the whiteboard, but one member's rankings have yet to be tallied. Finish tallying the votes and then identify the alternative the group should select as the best.

The current scores are: Source cheaper ingredients – 9, Reduce surplus supply of bread – 9, Make smaller loaves – 7, Work at night when electricity is cheaper – 6, Pack ovens better – 5, Stock up when prices are low – 4, Use cheaper packaging – 2, and Reduce staff – 0.

There is one more index card. It ranks the alternatives as follows: Work at night when electricity is cheaper – 3, Source cheaper ingredients – 1, and Reduce surplus supply of bread – 2.

Options:

1. Work at night when electricity is cheaper
2. Reduce surplus supply of bread
3. Reduce staff
4. Source cheaper ingredients

Answer

Option 1: This option is incorrect. You add the rankings from the last index card to the tally and then add up the score for each alternative. The alternative with the highest total score – in this case, producing less bread – is the best alternative.

Option 2: This is the correct option. You add the rankings from the last index card to the tally and total the score for each alternative. The idea of producing less bread gets a total of eleven points,

64. Problem-Solving and Decision-Making Strategies

which is the highest score.

Option 3: This option is incorrect. This alternative actually received the lowest number of votes. Remember that group members should be instructed to give the highest scores to the alternatives they think are best.

Option 4: This option is incorrect. When you add the last index card to the tally, this alternative gets a score of ten, which is not the highest total score.

Using ROI in Decision Making

ROI is a useful way of analyzing alternatives in terms of their impact on the bottom line. This is done by expressing in monetary terms all the costs and benefits associated with the alternatives for a particular decision. Even intangible costs and benefits are given an estimated cash value.

Once all the costs and benefits have been determined, you can divide the projected net return by the total investment and multiply the result by 100 to express the ROI as a percentage. This is one simple way to determine ROI for use in decision making.

The payback period is the period it takes for an investment to pay for itself. One way to calculate this is to divide the total projected cost of an alternative by the annual revenue it's expected to generate.

Including finance in decisions

Even in business, people sometimes forget to view their projects and decisions in terms of investments that are expected to generate monetary returns. Yet financial considerations are a top priority in many decision-making contexts. For example, decisions to expand globally, select products, train staff, and upgrade equipment all have a financial impact.

The importance of finance is most obvious when companies need to choose between alternatives that involve significant capital investments. In these cases, money is the bottom-line factor for determining which action should be taken.

Return on Investment – commonly known as ROI – calculations are perhaps the most popular financial measure of the merits of decision alternatives. So ROI is a key decision-making tool, especially in business situations.

ROI helps you evaluate and select alternatives based on their costs and benefits, so you use it during steps four and five of the decision-making process. Costs and benefits are expressed in dollars, or other units of currency, and then compared for each alternative.

It's challenging, but possible, to estimate the

monetary value of qualitative costs and benefits, such as staff morale, customer satisfaction, or a reputation for quality products or ethical actions. Though companies may not be able to measure qualitative variables precisely, they can firmly base their estimates on industry-accepted indices, rules of thumb, historical data, or benchmark data and norms.

Once all costs and benefits are given a monetary value, this common parameter can be used to measure and compare all the variables considered.

Question

How often do you think about financial costs and benefits when you make an important decision?

Options:

1. Often
2. Sometimes
3. Rarely

Answer

Option 1: If you deal directly with finances or are used to assessing decisions in relation to their financial impact, you'll be used to comparing likely returns to the investments required to generate them. Often the best choice is the most profitable one.

Option 2: You should always consider financial costs and benefits because they affect alternative

64. Problem-Solving and Decision-Making Strategies

solutions more often than you realize. You need to weigh decision alternatives by thinking about the returns they could generate in relation to the inputs required. ROI is a useful tool for making this type of assessment consciously and more accurately.

Option 3: Most people don't perform formal numerical ROI analyses when making everyday decisions. However, it's essential that when you're choosing among various decision alternatives, you mentally compare the inputs required to the returns they'll generate. Even if you don't deal directly with finance, the best choice in many situations is likely to be the one that's most profitable.

ROI helps you to compare ways to invest valuable resources, such as your time, money, and effort. This tool takes much of the guesswork out of decision making. People in leadership roles can use ROI to determine how an organization's resources should be spent, what goals to move toward, and what budget standards to create.

Question
Which statements do you think describe the benefits of using ROI calculations when making decisions?
Options:

Sorin Dumitrascu

1. Alternatives are compared with a common parameter

2. ROI values provide stakeholders with a rational and objective basis for determining the best alternative

3. ROI values enable stakeholders to measure the potential contribution of each alternative

4. ROI values help sponsors and executives to justify supporting financially-viable alternatives

5. Employees can focus on objective and tangible results when evaluating and implementing alternatives

6. Ethical considerations can be measured precisely when comparing alternatives 7. All uncertainty surrounding alternatives is eliminated

Answer

Option 1: This option is correct. ROI quantifies all types of costs and benefits – including qualitative and intangible ones – in terms of monetary value. This makes it possible to compare alternatives more easily, using a common, numerical parameter.

Option 2: This option is correct. Because ROI converts a multitude of different factors into monetary values, it gives stakeholders a rational and objective basis for comparing alternatives.

Option 3: This option is correct. Because returns for each alternative are expressed in terms of monetary values, they are quantifiable and measurable.

Option 4: This option is correct. ROI makes it possible to compare alternatives in terms of their bottom-line financial benefit. This information can be used to justify the choice of specific alternatives.

Option 5: This option is correct. It's easy for people to lose sight of important goals and get caught up in diversions. ROI helps employees stay focused on working towards financially profitable results when implementing chosen alternatives.

Option 6: This option is incorrect. Ethical considerations can't be measured precisely and objectively in an ROI analysis. However, companies can make an informed estimate of their effects.

Option 7: This option is incorrect. Using ROI to assess alternatives doesn't alter the risk or uncertainty associated with their outcomes.

Using ROI in decision making helps you to quantify information, calculate returns, and make rational and objective comparisons between decision alternatives. This tool is also useful when you inform leadership and justify the choice of specific alternatives, and it can help employees focus on tangible results.

Calculating ROI

An ROI value typically provides the ratio of the net return – or savings – of an alternative to the cost of the required investment. It can be written as a percentage. Total investment includes all the costs and expenditures required to implement the alternative. Net return is the profit you make over and above the costs of implementing the alternative. To calculate the ROI, you divide the net return by the total investment. Then you multiply your result by 100.

Of course, most decisions are made before the solution is implemented and before you have precise figures for returns and investment. So typically, the values you use in an ROI calculation will be anticipated or projected values, rather than actual returns. You'll estimate the net return and the investment to the best of your ability based on established trends, benchmarks, and other sources of information.

As a manager at a software company, you've been asked to calculate the ROI the company could expect if it markets a new Internet browser program. The first step you need to take is to establish revenue projections. Follow along as the calculation continues.

64. Problem-Solving and Decision-Making Strategies

Because many IT products quickly become outmoded, you decide to be cautious. You estimate how much revenue your company can expect to generate from the product over the next five years only. You create a table with three column headings: Year, Anticipated revenue, and Projected costs. One row is allocated to each year, and the last row is used to calculate totals.

When you calculate the expected revenue, you include intangible factors such as increased customer loyalty in your calculation. After careful analysis of customer profiles, you determine that this factor alone is worth $5,000 per year. This is in addition to $80,000 in income and $15,000 of revenue from other factors.

Including all relevant factors, you calculate that every year, your company can expect a revenue of $100,000 from the product, which gives a total of $500,000 over five years. You add $100,000 to each row in the anticipated revenue column for years 1 to 5. This comes to a total of $500,000.

Next you specify all projected costs, which comprise the total investment in the project. In this case, the major estimated expenditures are the development of the product itself, promotional costs, and additional administrative costs, for a total of

$400,000.

This is then entered into the Projected costs (Investment) column as a one-time expense.

The next step is to estimate the net return, which is the bottom-line profit you'll have after making all necessary expenditures to develop the new browser. To get this figure, you subtract the projected cost of $400,000 from the anticipated revenue of $500,000, for an estimated net return of $100,000.

Now that you have estimated the net return, you can use it to calculate the return on investment. To do this, you simply divide the net return of $100,000 by the projected costs – in other words, by the total investment of $400,000. Note that in some business contexts, total investment may include more than just the costs of implementation, but for purposes of this course, total costs and total investment are considered equal.

The net return of $100,000 is divided by the total investment of $400,000.

You then multiply the result by 100 to get a percentage. When you do this, you get an ROI of 25%. It seems the new Internet browser is well worth investing in. The net return of $100,000 is divided by the investment of $400,000 and then multiplied by 100 to give an ROI of 25%.

A higher ROI would be even more appealing. If,

64. Problem-Solving and Decision-Making Strategies

for instance, you calculated an ROI of 35% for another alternative, it should be favored over a project with only 25% ROI.

Time is a central factor when calculating ROI. Over five years, an ROI of 25% may be very good. But what if the browser becomes obsolete before five years have passed? Companies have to consider how long it will take for an investment to pay for itself.

This period is known as the payback period. The payback period helps to determine the level of risk involved in an investment. Before the payback period is reached, the total cost of an investment exceeds the total returns that it generates. It's only after the payback period ends that the company begins to earn money on its investment.

To calculate the payback period when the projected income is the same for each year, you divide the total amount of the investment by the annual revenue expected from the investment. In this example, the projected costs are $400,000 and annual revenue is $100,000. It will take four years for the revenue to equal the total investment. In other words, the new browser will pay for itself in four years.

Sorin Dumitrascu

Suppose your printing company has asked you to calculate the ROI and payback period for investing in a new black-and-white printing press. You've estimated the costs and revenues for the project over a ten-year period, and have taken care to include intangible benefits in your figures, such as the improvement in customer loyalty that will come from offering customers a wider variety of options.

Question

What are the ROI and the payback period in this situation?

The costs of the black-and-white printing press are projected at $160,000. It is expected to generate $20,000 revenue per year for ten years, which amounts to a total anticipated revenue of $200,000 and a net return of $40,000.

Options:

1. The ROI is 25% and the payback period is eight years 2. The ROI is 20% and the payback period is eight years 3. The ROI is 20% and the payback period is four years 4. The ROI is 25% and the payback period is four years

Answer

Option 1: This is the correct option. You divide the net return by the total investment and multiply the result by 100 to determine the ROI. To calculate

64. Problem-Solving and Decision-Making Strategies

the payback period, you divide the total investment by the annual revenue expected – in this case, $20,000. This gives you a payback period of eight years.

Option 2: This option is incorrect. To calculate the payback period, you divide the total investment by the expected annual revenue of $20,000. This gives a payback period of eight years, so this calculation is correct. However, to determine ROI, you divide the net return by the total investment and multiply the result by 100. The result is an ROI of 25%.

Option 3: This option is incorrect. To calculate the payback period, you divide the total investment by the annual revenue expected – in this case, $20,000. This gives a payback period of eight years. To determine ROI, you divide the net return by the total investment and multiply by 100. The result is an ROI of 25%.

Option 4: This option is incorrect. You divide the net return by the total investment and multiply the result by 100 to determine the ROI. In this case, $40,000 is 25% of $160,000, so your calculation is correct. However, to calculate the payback period, you divide the total investment by the annual revenue expected – in this case, $20,000. Doing this gives you a payback period of eight years.

Now suppose you're comparing three different printing presses to decide which represents the best investment for your company. You've decided to base your estimates of the costs and revenue that each press would generate on a ten-year period.

If you're deciding purely on the basis of payback period and the ROI, the alternative with the shortest payback period and the largest ROI is your best choice.

First you need to calculate the ROI for the three printing presses. For each of the three options, you divide the net return over a ten-year period by the total investment. Then you multiply the result by 100 to get the ROI percentage. For the color press, ROI is 11.11%, for the black-and-white press it is 25%, and for the newsprint press it is 100%.

To work out the payback period for each printing press, you divide the total cost by the annual revenue that it would generate.

Case Study: Question 1 of 1
Scenario

As a buyer, you have to choose between three different suppliers of T-shirts for the summer. You analyze sales figures and demographics over six years. You allocate monetary values to customer

64. Problem-Solving and Decision-Making Strategies

satisfaction, fashion sense, store reputation, and aesthetic appeal. You then assess the turnover of T-shirts in previous seasons and analyze possible mark-ups for three different suppliers:

Supplier A

Supplier A produces inexpensive T-shirts with a cut that appeals to heavier customers. However, the unattractive designs harm your reputation.

The total costs of purchasing from Supplier A is projected at $100,000. Stock is expected to generate $25,000 of revenue a month, which amounts to a net return of $50,000 over a six-month period.

Supplier B

Supplier B produces good quality, fashionable, but expensive T-shirts. They have a general appeal because they're well cut.

The total costs of the purchasing from Supplier B is projected at $150,000. Stock is expected to generate $50,000 of revenue a month, which amounts to a net return of $150,000 over a six-month period.

Supplier C

Supplier C produces up-market, reasonably priced T-shirts with an interesting cut and motif. This style will only appeal to teenage girls.

Sorin Dumitrascu

The total costs of the purchasing from Supplier C is projected at $120,000. Stock is expected to generate $25,000 of revenue a month, which amounts to a net return of $30,000 over a six-month period.

Question

Which supplier should you select, based on the ROI and payback period values?

Options:

1. Supplier B
2. Supplier A
3. Supplier C

Answer

Option 1: This is the correct option. Stocking supplier B's T-shirts for the summer offers a projected ROI of 100%, with a payback period of three months. So this supplier provides the highest ROI and the shortest payback period, making it the best choice.

Option 2: This option is incorrect. When you divide the net return of $50,000 by the investment of $100,000 for supplier A, you get an ROI of 50%. The payback period, which you calculate by dividing the investment of $100,000 by the monthly revenue of $25,000, is four months. Supplier B provides a higher ROI and a shorter payback period, making it the best supplier.

64. Problem-Solving and Decision-Making Strategies

Option 3: This option is incorrect. When you divide the net return of $30,000 by the investment of $120,000, you get an ROI of 25%. The payback period, derived by dividing the investment of $120,000 by the monthly revenue of $25,000, is 4.8 months. Supplier B provides a higher ROI and a shorter payback period, making it the best supplier.

Although the theory of calculating ROI is fairly straightforward, in practice there are numerous complexities to take into account. And there are various methods of calculating ROI to choose from, depending on your needs.

Revenues and expenditures may not be entirely predictable, and many situations require you to apply more complex and sensitive formulas. For example, you may need to calculate the future value of money, for which you would use Net Present Value calculations.

If the projected income and expenditure differs each year, you won't be able to determine the payback period by dividing total expenditure by the annual revenue. Instead, you need to sum the cumulative anticipated revenue and expenditure. The investment would be paid back when cumulative revenue becomes equal to cumulative expenditure.

Sorin Dumitrascu

Whatever methodology you choose, it's important that it have these characteristics:

- it's easy to use and straightforward enough to explain to others,
- it's comprehensive, clear, and meaningful enough to be used by top-level decision makers,
- it accurately accounts for all costs and profits, and
- it enables ROI values to be appropriately calculated for the particular business process in question.

Analysis Tools for Decision Making

A methodical decision-making process involves establishing a context for success, framing the issue properly, generating alternatives, evaluating the alternatives, and choosing the best alternative. Generating alternatives involves brainstorming ideas and ensuring proposed alternatives are broad, genuine, and feasible. Evaluating the alternatives involves analyzing their costs, benefits, risks, and relative feasibility.

You choose the best alternative by consolidating the results of evaluation, incorporating both subjective and objective information, and – in a group situation – reaching consensus or voting.

Devil's advocate technique

Many analysis tools are available to improve the way you make decisions. Three useful examples of these tools are the devil's advocate technique, plus-minus-interesting – or PMI – analysis, and the ease-and-effect matrix.

In a group situation, individuals' desire to conform and reach consensus can damage the decision- making process, especially at steps three, four, and five. The danger arises because of three factors to which groups are susceptible – groupthink, majority influence, and polarization.

Groupthink

With groupthink, the drive for consensus and group cohesion leads everyone to decide on a specific alternative before they've looked sufficiently at the options available.

Majority influence

The drive for conformity can lead to agreement on whatever the majority thinks is right. Participants with other views either don't voice them or are swayed by what the majority decides.

Polarization

If there's no dissent, it can polarize a decision. Views become more and more extreme because

64. Problem-Solving and Decision-Making Strategies

there are no conflicting perspectives to moderate them.

Question

In group settings, it can be difficult to disagree with others, even when you have different views. The difficulty arises from a need for conformity, a need to show loyalty to the group, and a need to reach the group's goals.

How often is there dissent in your decision-making meetings and discussions?

Options:
1. Often
2. Occasionally
3. Seldom

Answer

Option 1: Better decisions are often reached if dissent occurs in a safe setting. If the setting is not safe, too much conflict is generated and it becomes very difficult to reach any decision.

Option 2: If people are encouraged to dissent, you're likely to find that more creative and satisfying solutions are generated.

Option 3: If dissent seldom occurs, it may indicate participants are focusing too much on conforming. This makes creative ideas and solutions less likely.

Sorin Dumitrascu

If dissent is encouraged in a group setting, it helps to free people from the drive to conform. It also stimulates the search for information and helps members to tackle an issue from a range of perspectives. In turn, this encourages creative solutions. So even when opposing ideas are wrong or inappropriate, they can improve the decision-making process. The devil's advocate technique works on this premise.

To use the devil's advocate technique, you assign a person the role of devil's advocate. This person must then challenge group assumptions, question alternatives, bring in ideas previously not considered, and provide alternate perspectives or solutions. For this to be truly successful, the person you assign to the role should be experienced or an expert in the field.

Quite often, the devil's advocate's challenges will prompt decision makers to revise or reject their initial ideas in favor of more effective ones.

The technique is most helpful at stage four of the decision-making process, as alternatives are being evaluated.

Scott and Gail work for an interior decorator involved in the construction of a retirement home. They're currently discussing issues of safety. Follow

64. Problem-Solving and Decision-Making Strategies along as Scott plays the role of devil's advocate and prompts Gail to think of alternatives.

Gail: *We've created a coffee area over here, so residents can get themselves a hot drink and a snack. The garden and the lounge are close by.*

Scott: *What about people with movement disabilities? An ordinary kettle is too heavy and can be difficult to handle. It's easy for somebody to have an accident. Are you sure a coffee area is a good idea?*

Gail: *Well, of course we've designed the coffee area to be safe. We'll build a hot water system into the wall. You only have to push a lever to get hot water. We'll install rails at hip height to provide support and the floor will be covered with washable rubber matting.*

Scott: *That sounds much safer. But it also sounds more like a hospital than a home. Isn't it going to look too clinical?*

Gail: *Yes. I see what you mean. Well perhaps we could install wooden rails. And the rubber matting could have a print on it.*

Scott: *OK, that sounds better. Now tell me, why do you want to provide a coffee area at all?*

Question

Which statements from Gail and Scott's conversation represent use of the devil's advocate technique?

Options:

1. "Isn't it going to look too clinical?"
2. "It's easy for somebody to have an accident."
3. "Why do you want to provide a coffee area at all?"
4. "What about people with movement disabilities?"
5. "That sounds much safer."
6. "We've designed the coffee area to be safe."

Answer

The devil's advocate statements are those that raise new concerns, challenge existing assumptions, and critique the details of the proposal.

Option 1: This option is correct. Scott is questioning the alternative Gail proposes. This prompts Gail to respond to the new concern of the coffee area's look and feel.

Option 2: This is a correct option. By bringing the problem of potential accidents into the discussion, Scott focuses the discussion on safety as a major requirement in the coffee area.

Option 3: This option is correct. Scott is questioning the strongly held belief that a coffee area is beneficial. Gail then has to justify her position and think it through clearly.

Option 4: This option is correct. By bringing up

64. Problem-Solving and Decision-Making Strategies

issues that are not normally considered when designing a coffee area, Scott enriches the discussion and helps ensure all possibilities are covered.

Option 5: This option is incorrect. This statement doesn't challenge a suggestion and therefore isn't an example of using the devil's advocate technique.

Option 6: This option is incorrect. This statement is defensive rather than challenging. It's not an example of a person playing the role of devil's advocate.

By intentionally questioning or challenging the points Gail makes, Scott encourages deeper thought about the options. Ultimately, this is likely to result in the team making better decisions.

In fact, when ideas have been carefully critiqued and refined through devil's advocacy, decision-makers tend to find them more acceptable and satisfying.

PMI analysis

The PMI analysis tool builds and improves on the classic "pros and cons" analysis. It's useful in evaluating alternatives in step four of the decision-making model. Also, because it helps you decide whether an alternative is worth pursuing, it's particularly helpful as a final check once you've identified a preferred alternative in step five.

To perform PMI analysis, you use a table with three columns, labeled Plus, Minus, and Interesting. For example, you might use these columns to weigh the potential pros and cons of moving your store to a location across town.

Plus

You should add all the positive outcomes of taking a course of action to the Plus column and assign a numerical value to each based on its importance.

For example, one benefit of the new location is better access for drop-in customers. Because you feel this is a moderately important benefit, you assign it a positive value of six. You assign a positive value of four to more parking. The total of the Plus column is ten.

Minus

64. Problem-Solving and Decision-Making Strategies

In the Minus column, you enter all the negative outcomes of taking a course of action. These outcomes can also be assigned numeric values.

For example, you give higher rent a value of minus four and moving costs a value of minus two. The total of the Minus column is therefore minus six.

Interesting

In the Interesting column, you enter any further implications of following the given alternative. The implications may be positive or negative in their outcomes.

For example, you may suffer a minor loss of customers due to the move so you give this possibility a score of minus four. On the other hand, there's less competition in the new neighborhood, which you decide to give a positive value of four. The total for this column adds to zero.

Typically, the Interesting column is reserved for the long-term implications of an alternative or its impact on areas of the organization other than those you are directly concerned with.

It's not always necessary to assign each factor a value or weight to represent its impact on the situation. Sometimes, just listing the relevant plus, minus, and interesting factors can make it obvious what you should decide.

But weighting the factors can clarify a decision. If you do assign values, be aware the scoring system you choose is subjective, based simply on how you judge the importance of each factor relative to the others under consideration.

If you chose a scale of one to ten, for instance, you'd give factors with a negligible impact a score of one and those with a very strong impact a score of ten.

In a weighted PMI analysis, your final total score for a decision doesn't just indicate a "yes" or "no" – it also indicates your level of certainty. A large negative or positive suggests you should strongly endorse or strongly disapprove the relevant course of action. In other words, smaller numbers indicate less confidence in the conclusion.

In the example PMI analysis, you want to know whether the positives of moving your store outweigh the negatives. To find out, you simply add the column totals. Ten plus negative six plus zero equals positive four. This total tells you that moving the store is a good alternative, but doesn't come with very strong certainty.

Ease-and-effect matrix

After turning in your master's thesis, your professor points out you repeatedly used the wrong referencing format. What do you do? It's simple – you correct the formatting for references. You certainly don't rewrite your entire thesis based on new references. That alternative is neither easy nor effective.

Prioritizing business decisions works in much the same way. You should generally prioritize solutions that are both easy and effective. The ease-and-effect matrix is useful for evaluating a number of alternatives at the same time, based on their effectiveness in achieving the desired result and their ease of implementation. It's a suitable tool during step four of the decision-making model – evaluating alternatives.

Question

What do you think is the highest priority area of the ease-and-effect matrix?

The ease-and-effect matrix has three columns and three rows. The row headers are Very easy, Moderate, and Difficult. The column headers are Very effective, Moderate, and Ineffective. Alternative 1 is in the Very easy, Very effective cell, Alternatives 2 and 4 are in the Moderate, Very easy cell. Alternative 3 is in the Very easy, Ineffective cell. Alternative 5 is placed in the Moderate, Very effective cell, Alternative 6 is in the Moderate, Moderate cell. Alternative 7 is in the Moderate, Ineffective cell. Alternative 8 is in the Difficult, Very effective cell, Alternative 9 is in the Difficult, Moderate cell, Alternative 10 is in the Difficult, Ineffective cell.

Options:
1. The Very easy, Very effective cell
2. The Moderate effective and Very Easy cell
3. The Difficult and Ineffective cell

Answer

Option 1: Alternatives that are both very easy and very effective have the highest priority. Other high-priority cells include the Moderate easy and Very effective cell, and the Very easy and Moderate effective cell.

Option 2: Although this cell holds the most options, very easy and very effective options have the highest priority.

Option 3: Difficult and ineffective options have the lowest priority. The very easy and very effective options have the highest priority.

Suppose you're deciding what to do about a

64. Problem-Solving and Decision-Making Strategies

supplier of glass doors who isn't delivering goods on time.

You've generated a number of alternatives and you want to compare them. To create an ease-and-effect matrix, you first rate each alternative on ease and then on effectiveness. Next you plot the alternatives on the matrix. Finally, you prioritize alternatives based on their positions within the matrix.

Rate ease of each alternative

First you rate each alternative based on its ease of implementation. Will it be easy, moderate, or difficult to implement?

Ending the relationship with the supplier who delivers late is the easiest solution, so you assign it the "very easy" rating. Bartering with the supplier for discounts on late items requires some negotiation, so you assign it a "moderate" rating. It requires a great deal of time and work for you to pick up the glass doors from the supplier instead of waiting for delivery, because they are bulky, heavy, and fragile. So this potential solution gets a rating of "difficult."

Rate effectiveness of each alternative

As the second step, you rate each alternative on effectiveness.

Ending the relationship is feasible, but you'd have to find a new supplier. It wouldn't effectively solve your problem, so this option gets a rating of "ineffective." Picking up the supplies won't solve the problem because it's just as time consuming and expensive as waiting for delivery, so this idea gets a rating of "ineffective."

Bartering for discounts is a good way of improving your business relationship and saving money. You decide to give it a rating of "very effective."

Plot alternatives on matrix

You plot the alternatives on the ease-and-effect matrix, according to their assigned ratings.

Barter is in the moderately easy and very effective cell. End relationship is in the very easy and but ineffective cell. Pick up supplies is in the difficult and ineffective cell.

Prioritize alternatives

Once the alternatives are mapped out on the matrix, it's easy to see which are preferable. The matrix can be divided into three color-coded areas of three cells each. The areas are then used to rank the alternatives into three levels of priority – high, medium, and low.

The high priority zone consists of the three cells that contain the optimum alternatives. The option to barter with the supplier falls into this zone. The medium priority zone encompasses moderately appealing alternatives, including the option of ending your relationship with the supplier. The low-priority zone is made up of the three least appealing positions. Picking up the supplies yourself belongs here.

Based on this ease-and-effect matrix, bartering for discounts emerges as the best alternative.

The high priority area contains the very easy and very effective cell, the moderately easy and very effective cell, and the very easy and moderately effective cell.

The medium priority area contains the very easy but ineffective cell, the moderately easy and moderately effective cell, and the difficult but very effective cell.

The low priority area contains the moderately easy but ineffective cell, the difficult and ineffective cell, and the difficult but moderately effective cell.

The ease-and-effect matrix doesn't always produce a clear winner. You may have to decide whether it's more important that an alternative be easy to implement or effective in bringing about a desired outcome.

Also, it's not always clear how you should rate

an alternative. If you aren't sure how easy or effective an alternative will be, you may want to revise and reassess its pros and cons. You may also find it useful to ask what could be done to make a particular alternative easier or more effective, then redefine the alternative accordingly.

Because of this changeable quality of the ease-and-effect matrix, you can write alternatives on sticky notes, which you then move around the matrix.

Question

Match the characteristics to the corresponding decision-making tools. Each tool may have more than one match.

Options:

A. Reduces the likelihood of decisions being too extreme

B. Clarifies the pros and cons of a decision

C. Weighs the effort required to implement a decision and its overall impact

D. Involves placing alternatives spatially to compare their relative priorities

E. Often involves determining a numerical value for an alternative

F. Encourages debate about alternatives

Targets:

64. Problem-Solving and Decision-Making Strategies

1. Devil's advocate technique
2. PMI analysis
3. Ease-and-effect matrix

Answer

The devil's advocate technique reduces the likelihood of polarization and groupthink. It involves assigning someone specifically to challenge ideas and encourage debate about alternatives.

PMI analysis clarifies the benefits and drawbacks for an alternative. Each pro and con can be assigned weighted numerical values, giving a total value for the alternative.

The ease-and effect-matrix plots the effort required to implement a decision against its overall impact or effectiveness. This is done by placing options spatially across a matrix.

Decision Making: Making Tough Decisions

Dealing with Uncertainty in Decision Making

Compromises and Trade-offs in Decision Making

Using Your Intuition in Decision Making

Dealing with Uncertainty in Decision Making

Making decisions in uncertain conditions can be difficult. The best approach in these cases is to begin by identifying and quantifying the unknowns.

Next, you should prioritize areas of uncertainty based on their potential impact on a decision's outcome.

Finally, it's important to reduce key uncertainties. Strategies for doing this include acquiring relevant knowledge, reducing the time gap between making a decision and realizing its outcome, taking risk–reducing steps during the implementation of a decision, and creating contingency plans.

Uncertainty and its different levels

Statistician George Chacko said that uncertainty is the "commitment of resources today for results tomorrow." This type of uncertainty is often a factor in decision making. Because you can't predict the future, you can't always know for certain how a choice you make will play out, or which of several alternatives will prove to be the best.

So uncertainty complicates decisions. It means having to factor unknowns into the decision-making process.

Also, it's natural for people to try to avoid uncertainty, and this tendency can compromise the decision- making process. It can lead decision makers to cling to alternatives already tried in the past, or to go with

inferior decisions because their likely outcomes appear more certain.

Say a transport company is doing well and its managers are thinking about expanding the business. They can estimate the returns this will yield over the next year, but not without guesswork.

Uncertainties

Changes in the market, increases in the price of fuel, and actions taken by the company's

64. Problem-Solving and Decision-Making Strategies

competitors affect the outcome of the decision. These factors are uncertain.

Other, less directly related factors also introduce uncertainty. For instance, a few months after implementing a decision to expand, the company loses its biggest client due to unforeseen circumstances. Managers couldn't have predicted this event, but it may jeopardize the success of their decision.

Now consider a personal decision to purchase a new home. Changes you can't predict in the property market and in the area you plan to buy in may significantly change the value of your investment over the coming years.

Also, you may not know whether you'll be able to sell your existing home in time to invest in the new property. And, at a more personal level, you can't know for certain that you'll be happy in the new neighborhood.

Decisions you need to make can involve different levels of uncertainty:

- they may involve uncertainty about a single outcome – for example, if it's uncertain whether the result of a course of action will be positive or negative,
- they may involve uncertainty about a few

outcomes,
- they may involve uncertainty about a wide range of possible outcomes, or
- they may involve complete uncertainty.

When you make a decision in uncertain conditions, you're essentially taking a risk.

It's not possible to avoid this risk completely. But what you can do is prepare properly and take steps to reduce the risk of your decision.

Identifying areas of uncertainty

In business, most decision making involves some uncertainty. To make the best decisions without taking unnecessary risks, you need to confront the unknowns, analyze and understand the uncertainty that's involved as far as possible, and then take what steps you can to reduce the uncertainty. Then you need to act, based on the best information you have.

So to tackle uncertainty head-on in your decision making, you should follow this series of steps:

1. identify the unknowns – or areas of uncertainty – affecting your decision and quantify these

2. prioritize the unknowns that you've identified, and

3. take steps to reduce key uncertainties that affect your decision to minimize the associated risks

Question

Sequence the steps for tackling uncertainty head-on.

Options:

A. Identify unknowns
B. Prioritize unknowns
C. Reduce key uncertainties

Answer

Identify unknowns is ranked the first step. First, you tackle uncertainty head-on by identifying the unknowns affecting the possible outcome of a decision.

Prioritize unknowns is ranked the second step. Once you've determine the unknowns, you prioritize them so you know where it's best to focus your efforts to reduce uncertainty.

Reduce key uncertainties is ranked the third step. Finally, you tackle uncertainty head-on to reduce key uncertainties.

The first step is to identify the areas where uncertainty exists. Put simply, if you don't know where or what the risks are, you can't take steps to address them.

However, it's only once you've reached the evaluation stage of the decision-making process that you should work on identifying areas of uncertainty. If you do this at an earlier stage, you're likely to stifle the creativity needed to generate a set of viable alternatives.

One way to identify areas of uncertainty is to brainstorm, either individually or in a group, to come up with a list of all the possible uncertainties that could affect a decision's outcome. Some

64. Problem-Solving and Decision-Making Strategies

examples of uncertainties may be changes in fashion trends, consumer spending habits, cash flow, and competitors' actions.

For example, a computer game company wants to introduce a new game controller to its line. It has designed three alternative controllers, and managers now need to choose which of the three prototypes to implement. The first thing they do is brainstorm a list of uncertainties. They include targeted market share, expected annual unit sales, unit production costs, competitors' actions, and expected unit sales price.

After brainstorming for uncertainties, you attempt to quantify them. A good way to do this is to express each uncertainty as a possible range of values.

This range of uncertainty, as opposed to providing just an initial estimate, leaves room for variation. Having only a single-point estimate wouldn't leave room for any variation and could throw subsequent budgeting out, whereas providing a range leaves room for variation.

When you're in the process of determining estimates as ranges, it's important to consult others who can help you make the estimates as accurate as possible. The managers of the computer game company, for example, consult suppliers for price estimates and a project manager who has completed a similar project for advice.

Sometimes it's not possible to express an uncertainty as a range. For instance, the computer gaming company's main competitor either will or won't launch a similar controller. In this case, a single estimate like a percentage can be used to indicate a confidence level.

Managers at the computer game company work out three probabilities per prototype relating to how their competitors will react to the release of the new game controller – the likelihood that the competitors will bring out a similar product, that the company's product sales will be affected, and that the new product will fail to recover its cost. By multiplying these probabilities, you quantify the uncertainty and get an end result that shows how probable it is that the product will fail to recover its cost.

Question

A project team identifies a range of uncertainties while planning the construction of a new conveyor belt. The team doesn't approach experts before assigning estimates.

How can it improve its handling of uncertainties?

The uncertainties are installation cost, downtime,

64. Problem-Solving and Decision-Making Strategies

increased sales, increased production, and competitors' actions. Installation cost is estimated at $4,000, downtime is estimated at 2 weeks, increased sales is estimated at 5%, increased production is estimated at 60%, and competitors' actions might have an effect.

Options:
1. Express each uncertainty as a value range
2. Give competitors' actions a confidence value
3. Consult experts to review the estimates
4. Express the confidence level as a range
5. Express competitors' actions in a range

Answer

Option 1: This is a correct option. The team should express the estimates of the uncertainties as ranges, rather than as single-point percentages or values. This will clarify the extent of each uncertainty and leave room for variation.

Option 2: This option is correct. If the team can't express competitors' actions – an uncertainty – as a range, it can assign a confidence value. This probability rating tells the team how the uncertainty may impact the decision's outcome.

Option 3: This is a correct option. To get its estimates as accurate as possible, the team should consult others with relevant knowledge or experience.

Option 4: This option is incorrect. The confidence level in a particular estimate doesn't have to be expressed as a range – a percentage value is generally appropriate.

Option 5: This is an incorrect option. The competitors' actions can't be expressed as a range because they either will or won't happen. In this case, the team should add a confidence value by working out the probability.

Prioritizing the unknowns

The second step in tackling uncertainty head-on is to prioritize the unknowns you've identified, based on the extent to which they're likely to impact the outcome of a decision.

This involves three steps – gauging the impact of each unknown, prioritizing the unknowns according to their impact, and identifying and clarifying the impact of unknowns that may work together.

Once the uncertainties have been identified, you need to determine what kind of impact each uncertainty may have on the outcome of your decision.

For the computer game company, for example, uncertainties surrounding market share and unit sales price are likely to have the greatest impact on a decision to launch a new game controller.

Once you've determined the potential impact of each uncertainty, you can compare and prioritize them according to their impact on the company.

So in the case of the computer company, the managers reorder the uncertainties into a prioritized list. Top priorities are the uncertainties of the market share and the unit sales price. They place the expected annual unit sales as their second priority, followed by competitors' actions, and finally, the unit production costs.

Another approach is to clarify the impact of uncertainties that may work together. To get a result for the combined uncertainties, you multiply the two values.

For example, the managers want to get an idea of the expected revenues for each prototype so they multiply the expected annual unit sales by the expected unit sales price.

To get a range of the revenue for each prototype, they multiply the lowest possible number of sales by the lowest possible sales price, and then the highest possible number of sales by the highest possible sales price. The revenue for prototype A lies anywhere between $1,000,000 and $1,750,000. The unit production costs have not yet been subtracted from this range.

Question

What are appropriate activities for the second step of dealing with uncertainty in decision making?

Options:

1. Establish the impact each uncertainty may have on the outcome of your decision
2. Reorder the unknowns into a prioritized list
3. Clarify the impact of unknowns that may interact by multiplying their values

64. Problem-Solving and Decision-Making Strategies

4. Prioritize the uncertainties that are more easily dealt with

5. Prioritize the unknowns according to how immediate their effect will be

Answer

Option 1: This is a correct option. By establishing the impact of each uncertainty on the outcome of your decision, you're able to prioritize the uncertainties.

Option 2: This option is correct. When dealing with uncertainties, it's useful to list and prioritize them according to their impact. This way, you can put the uncertainties that have the most impact on your decision first. This helps you reduce the overall level of uncertainty for your decision.

Option 3: This is a correct option. It's sometimes useful to combine the uncertainties that link to each other because it provides you with more information about your alternatives. When you want to clarify the impact of interacting uncertainties, you multiply them. For example, you multiply the expected number of unit sales and the expected value per unit to get a revenue range.

Option 4: This option is incorrect. You should give priority to those uncertainties that will have the most impact on your decision, even if they're difficult to tackle. If you only deal with the easiest factors, you won't improve your level of uncertainty very much.

Option 5: This is an incorrect option. You should prioritize those uncertainties that will have the most impact on your decision. The unknowns that have more of an immediate effect aren't necessarily the ones that will have the most impact on your decisions.

Reducing uncertainty

Once you've prioritized the areas of uncertainty surrounding a decision, you're in a position to move on to step three – reducing key uncertainties or the uncertainties you've identified as having the highest priorities or the lowest confidence estimates.

The final step in handling key uncertainties surrounding a decision is to reduce these uncertainties as much as possible. Several strategies help you do this.

One of the primary strategies is simply acquiring relevant knowledge to reduce – or even possibly eliminate – uncertainty before you make a final decision.

To acquire relevant knowledge in an attempt to reduce uncertainty, you can choose to use these strategies:

- conducting customer research in the appropriate market,
- inviting a wide range of people from different backgrounds to participate in group discussions about the product,
- evaluating customers' previous experiences and satisfaction with a similar product,
- conducting appropriate product testing and quality checks,

- creating and testing a simulation or model of the product, and
- seeking additional information from others who have knowledge about the decision or experience with a similar one.

In addition to various strategies, you may use a variety of tools and predictive models to help reduce the uncertainty surrounding decisions. Examples of these are statistical, mathematical, econometric, and software-based tools.

Acquiring the right knowledge can reduce or even eliminate uncertainty. However, it's not always possible or practical to obtain this knowledge.

In some cases, it's not even desirable, because you may gain an advantage by working under conditions of uncertainty. For example, making a decision before trying to combat every uncertainty could decrease your time-to-market, enabling you to beat your competitors.

The most important thing is to manage uncertainty effectively. Instead of trying to eliminate it entirely before you make decisions, you can follow three steps. You can bring the "horizon" closer by reducing the time it takes to implement a decision, take risk-reducing steps when a decision is already being implemented, and create effective contingency plans.

64. Problem-Solving and Decision-Making Strategies

Bringing the horizon closer means reducing the time gap between making a decision and realizing its consequences. This can reduce uncertainty simply because the near future is easier to predict than the distant future. For example, getting a new product to market quickly makes it less likely that market conditions will have changed before the product becomes available.

Another approach is to take risk-reducing steps during the implementation of a decision. This could, for example, involve using probation periods for newly hired staff if it's a hiring decision or implementing a decision in stages if the decision is about whether or not to develop a new product.

Probationary periods

Having new staff complete probation periods enables companies to make initial hiring decisions that are highly uncertain, and then to finalize these decisions only once the uncertainty has been reduced.

Implementing a decision in stages

When you implement a decision in stages, you need to review the outcome of each stage before moving to the next. This is sometimes referred to as a stage-gate system.

For example, you review a decision to invest in a

project after each of several stages, including research, design, and testing. After each stage, you either make necessary adjustments or discontinue the investment. This reduces risk because much greater losses are likely if you continue with a bad decision to the end.

As a final step for handling uncertainty surrounding decisions, it's imperative that you create contingency plans. This involves envisioning what could go wrong and planning how to respond if it does. This helps ensure that if a risk is realized, you'll be prepared to deal with it efficiently.

Even using all the available strategies for handling uncertainty can't generally eliminate it altogether. However, these strategies can help you reduce its extent and, as a result, make more effective decisions.

Question

What are examples of valid strategies for reducing key uncertainties in decision making?

Options:

1. Jonas develops a backup plan that requires 24-hour shift work in case employees reject his plan to introduce overtime

2. Valerie reduces production time to beat

64. Problem-Solving and Decision-Making Strategies

competitors

3. Dave is nervous about production, so he divides the project into stages, with a review after each stage

4. Samantha cuts out the uncertainties that are most difficult to deal with when hiring a new employee

5. Rachel introduces probationary periods for new employees when making a hiring decision

6. Carlos conducts research before developing a prototype

7. Claude extends the launch date of the new product as he is not sure of changing consumer requirements

Answer

Option 1: This option is correct. Backup plans – or contingency plans – detail how you'll respond to particular risks if they're realized. In this case, Jonas has an alternative plan to implement if employees reject his overtime package. This reduces the likely impact of the risks.

Option 2: This is a correct option. By cutting down production time, Valerie is essentially moving the horizon closer, which means there's less time for things to go wrong.

Option 3: This option is correct. Implementing a decision in stages and conducting a review after every stage can significantly reduce uncertainty. After each stage, Dave can make the necessary adjustments, or even choose to discontinue production entirely.

Option 4: This option is incorrect. The uncertainties that are most difficult to deal with may have the most impact on Samantha's decision. In this case, the risks need to be prioritized and dealt with.

Option 5: This is a correct option. By introducing probationary periods, Rachel reduces the risks associated with hiring new employees.

Option 6: This option is correct. It may be possible for Carlos to reduce, or even eliminate, uncertainty by obtaining additional information before making a final decision.

Option 7: This is an incorrect option. It's preferable to shorten the time it takes to implement an uncertain decision as much as possible. This can mean there's less time for things to change or to go wrong.

Compromises and Trade-offs in Decision Making

Decisions are especially complex when you need to evaluate alternatives in terms of multiple objectives because you'll often need to make compromises, or trade-offs. In these cases, using a methodical system can help you narrow down the alternatives to identify the best one.

First you need to create a consequence matrix, listing alternatives and objectives. You then quantify or rank the consequence of each alternative on how well it meets each objective.

Next, you eliminate obviously weak alternatives and any objectives for which the remaining alternatives have tied scores.

You then make trade-offs and compromises to arrive at the best decision.

Decision making and trade-offs

You can think of a trade-off as a compromise. In decision making, people often compromise. They may opt for an alternative that's less than ideal for a variety of reasons. For example, a compromise may be convenient, serve vested interests, ensure approval of a decision by superiors, or simply represent the path of least resistance. It may also make the decision maker look good or even provide this person with a means of saving face if something goes wrong with a decision later.

In all these examples, compromising involves going with a decision that is not based on a rational, fact-driven evaluation that identifies the best alternative. More often than not, they simply rely on gut feelings,
common sense, and guesswork.

But there is another kind of compromise that's not just a "convenient" or "easy-way-out" option. This type of trade-off doesn't involve guesswork and instead provides a practical way of making trade-offs across a range of alternatives.

Consider John, who's currently trying to decide between two job offers. Job A offers a larger salary but comes with only a six-month contract. It's with a more prestigious company and may enhance his job

64. Problem-Solving and Decision-Making Strategies

prospects, but it'll require a longer commute. Job B offers better long-term security, a shorter commute, and better health benefits.

Like in John's case, it can be difficult to decide on the optimum trade-off between objectives when you've got to make a decision that involves compromise.

This is because you measure different objectives using different scales. For example, John may make a subjective decision about which criteria are the most important to him when choosing a job offer. But how can he compare the two offers and then determine which offer is best in a more rational way?

When making decisions, the problem is often that it's difficult to compare different objectives in separate categories. It's rather like trying to compare two fractions – for example, four-fifths and three-quarters.

What's needed is a single scale for indicating how well each alternative meets each objective. Once you've got a common system of measurement, it becomes easier to compare values and so to make the best trade-offs. Applying this system to your fractions, you work with the common denominator of 20, making it much easier to identify the larger fraction.

Sorin Dumitrascu

A basic methodology that can help you make rational trade-offs comprises three steps. First you create a consequence matrix, with a single scale for ranking how well each alternative meets each objective. Next you eliminate weaker alternatives. And finally, you use the results to make logical trade-offs between the objectives.

Using this methodology doesn't mean that you won't have to make tough choices, but it simplifies the process of evaluating and comparing alternatives.

It also helps ensure that when you do make choices, they're based on a rational process that identifies the best trade-offs.

Step 1: Create a consequence matrix

Before considering trade-offs, you should have a clear idea of the decision at hand. You need to know your alternatives and the objectives you want to fulfill, and then determine how each alternative affects each objective – or determine its consequence.

Recording and making sense of this information can be a daunting task, especially when many alternatives and objectives are involved.

This is where a consequence matrix comes in. It enables you to list alternatives and objectives in a manageable format and rank the consequences of each alternative in terms of each objective using a single scale.

Consider Tina, who's an event coordinator. She needs to choose one of four catering companies to cater for an executive end-of-year party. She'll have to make some trade-offs, and wants them to be sound. She starts the process by creating a consequence matrix, listing her alternatives and specific objectives.

Alternatives

Tina enters the alternatives available as column headers of the consequence matrix.

Her alternatives are four different catering companies, so she creates four columns, headed Caterer A, Caterer B, Caterer C, and Caterer D.

Objectives

Tina considers the objectives she wants a catering company to satisfy. She then lists each objective in the row headers of the consequence matrix.

In this case, she identifies six objectives. Ideally, the chosen company should cater for vegetarian, low sodium, and gluten-free diets, offer the lowest cost per person, and provide a clean-up service as part of the overall cost. Tina would prefer not to have to provide any equipment, and the company's reputation is important. No one company is likely to emerge as the best in all these categories, so Tina has to make trade-offs as part of the decision-making process.

Once Tina has recorded the relevant alternatives and objectives, she can rate how well each alternative satisfies each objective. For each objective, she can use a qualitative system, describing each consequence in words, or a quantitative system, assigning a numeric value – like a dollar amount – to each objective.

64. Problem-Solving and Decision-Making Strategies

Whichever approach she decides to use, though, it's important to be consistent across each objective. Values that are qualitative can't be compared with those that are quantitative, hence the need for Tina to make some changes. For example, she shouldn't compare a reputation based on the quantitative value of 40% with the qualitative reputation of a verbal value – good, best, and fair. So she changes 40% to poor. Likewise, she updates the cost per person so they all reflect the quantitative dollar values.

Creating a consequence matrix forces Tina to identify all relevant alternatives and objectives. It also enables her to order her thoughts and arrange the information that should influence her decision in a concise format.

It also makes it much easier for her to compare the different alternatives in terms of each of her objectives.

If your decision involves many alternatives and objectives, it can result in a lot of descriptive information in a consequence matrix.

This can make it tricky to figure out which alternative is the best overall.

So it's a good idea to rank the consequences, according to how well they fulfill a given objective. For instance, if a particular alternative meets an objective best, Tina gives it a ranking of 1. Then she identifies the second-best alternative and gives it a ranking of 2. She uses the ranking of 4 to describe an alternative that doesn't meet an objective.

Question

Access the learning aid Lauren's Consequence Matrix to review a consequence matrix.

Then match the decision objectives to the corresponding rankings in the matrix.

Options:

A. Monthly salary
B. Vacation entitlement
C. Pension benefits
D. Healthcare benefits

Targets:

1. 3, 1, 1, 2
2. 1, 3, 4, 2
3. 1, 3, 2, 1
4. 1, 1, 2, 1

Answer

In Lauren's consequence matrix, she's ranked the monthly salary of Job A as 3, Job B as 1, of Job C as 1, and of Job D as 2. So the ranking sequence for monthly salary is 3, 1, 1, 2.

In the matrix, Lauren has ranked the vacation entitlement for Job A as 1, for Job B as 3, for Job C

64. Problem-Solving and Decision-Making Strategies

as 4, and for Job D as 2. So the ranking sequence for vacation entitlement is 1, 3, 4, 2.

In Lauren's consequence matrix, she's ranked pension benefits for Job A as 1, for Job B as 3, for Job C as 2, and for Job D as 1. So the ranking sequence for pension benefits is 1, 3, 2, 1.

In the matrix, Lauren has ranked healthcare benefits for Job A as 1, for Job B as 1, for Job C as 2, and for Job D as 1. So the ranking sequence for pension benefits is 1, 1, 2, 1.

Step 2: Eliminate weaker alternatives

Once you've created a consequence matrix, the next step is to eliminate weaker alternatives. To do this, you compare the rankings in the columns of the matrix.

Lower values indicate better alternatives, so in this example, Alternative C is clearly a better option than Alternative B.

If a particular alternative is worse in relation to all objectives than another alternative, you can eliminate it straight away. This is because it's clearly a weaker alternative.

You can take this a step further – if one alternative is weaker or the same as another alternative on all but one objective, and you judge that objective to be of minor value to you and your decision, you can remove that alternative.

By removing weaker alternatives, you're left with fewer options, simplifying the process of making a decision and ensuring you're making fewer trade-offs.

Consider how Tina should go about eliminating weaker alternatives in the consequence matrix she's compiled. Given the rankings she's applied for each caterer, which are the dominant and weak alternatives?

64. Problem-Solving and Decision-Making Strategies

Caterer A

According to Tina's consequence matrix, caterer A's ratings across all objectives are 3, 2, 1, 3, and 2.

When considering the ratings and consequences of caterer A on Tina's objectives, it's clear that this is a relatively weak alternative.

Caterer B

In her consequence matrix, Tina's assigned caterer B the following ratings across all the objectives: 1, 3, 1, 3, and 4.

Overall, by considering these ratings, it appears that caterer B is a weak alternative.

Caterer C

The ratings for caterer C across the objectives are 2, 1, 1, 2, and 1.

If you consider the consequences of caterer C on Tina's objectives, it seems a very strong alternative. And when comparing it to the other alternatives, it becomes apparent that it's dominant over caterer A, because in all rows, its rankings are higher than or equal to caterer A's.

Caterer D

The ratings for caterer D on each of the objectives in the consequence matrix are 1, 2, 1, 1, and 3.

This alternative is very strong and, when

compared to caterer B, is the dominant alternative, because in all rows, its rankings are higher than or equal to caterer B's.

By comparing the ranking values for the alternatives, Tina determines that caterers C and D are much better options than caterers A or B, so she eliminates the two weaker alternatives. She now needs to decide between the two stronger alternatives.

Question

David needs to decide which of four Internet service providers – commonly known as ISPs – will best meet his company's needs. So he creates a consequence matrix with three objectives – monthly cost, initial connection fee, and help-desk support and maintenance. He includes rankings to indicate how well each alternative meets each objective.

Which two alternatives can David eliminate?

In the consequence matrix, for the objective "Monthly cost," the alternative ISP A rates a 1, ISP B a 2, ISP C a 1, and ISP D a 2. For the objective "Initial connection fee," ISP A rates a 2, ISP B a 1, ISP C a 3, and ISP D a 1. For the objective "Helpdesk support and maintenance," ISP A rates a 1, ISP B a 2, ISP C a 2, and ISP D a 3.

64. Problem-Solving and Decision-Making Strategies

Options:
1. ISP B
2. ISP D
3. ISP A
4. ISP C

Answer

Option 1: This is an incorrect option. ISP B has been ranked higher overall than ISPs C and D, so it's a relatively strong alternative.

Option 2: This option is correct. ISP D has been ranked lower than ISP A and ISP B, so it can be eliminated as a weaker alternative.

Option 3: This is an incorrect option. ISP A has been given higher rankings overall than both ISP C and ISP D, so it shouldn't be eliminated as a weaker alternative.

Option 4: This option is correct. ISP C has been ranked lower overall than ISPs A and B, so it should be eliminated as a weaker alternative.

Step 3: Make trade-offs

So you've created a consequence matrix that details specific objectives, alternatives, and the consequences that each alternative has on an objective.

You've then used this information to assess all alternatives and to eliminate those that are weaker.

At this stage in the decision-making process, you may be left with only a single alternative that clearly dominates all the others. If so, your decision is straightforward.

However, this often isn't the case. It's more likely that after the elimination stage, you'll be left with more than one alternative to choose from – each with its own advantages and disadvantages.

Now you're confronted with the task of making a choice – not by eliminating alternatives, or columns, but by artificially eliminating objectives, or rows, from the matrix.

You have to make trade-offs between objectives. First, you can eliminate an objective whose alternatives contain the same consequence, because it won't determine what the best alternative is.

Say you're deciding between two medical aid providers, which you've identified as the best alternatives out of an original set of five. In this case, you've recorded actual values rather than rankings. Because both providers offer yearly medical savings of up to $10,000, it makes sense at this stage to eliminate the medical savings objective.

Once you've eliminated objectives with the same consequences, you have to deal with the remaining objectives. To do this, it's best to follow a four-step process:
- determine what change would eliminate an objective,
- determine what change in another objective would compensate for the elimination make the necessary switch, and
- remove the canceled objective.

Once Tina has eliminated the weaker alternatives, she eliminates the objective for which the remaining alternatives are tied – in this case, the objective "Is a clean-up service part of the overall cost?" Tina now takes the first two steps to make a trade-off between the first objective, concerned with diet, and the second objective, which relates to cost.

First objective
Tina investigates the objective of finding a caterer that can provide vegetarian, low sodium, and gluten-free meals.

For caterer C, Tina would have to purchase gluten-free meals for a small number of guests from another vendor. She determines that this will add an extra $2.50 to the total cost per person. So she eliminates the objective dealing with the selection of diets and adds $2.50 to the cost of using caterer C. This brings the price up to $18.50 per person.

Second objective

Tina considers the objective of finding the caterer that offers the lowest cost per person.

If Tina chooses caterer C, she'll have to rent cutlery at a cost of $1 per person. This information lets Tina eliminate the objective associated with equipment rental. She compensates this loss by adding $1 to the cost per person for caterer C. So the matrix now shows that caterer C will cost $16 per person. Caterer D provides all equipment, so the cost remains at $25 per person.

Tina is now left with only two objectives – cost per person and reputation – for comparing caterers C and D. Caterer C will cost $18.50 and has the best reputation. Caterer D will cost $25 and has a fair reputation.

With a consequence matrix, Tina's decision to hire caterer C proves to be an easy one. However,

64. Problem-Solving and Decision-Making Strategies

it's not always possible to quantify consequences in terms of costs. And you may not always be left with only one, obviously preferable alternative.

Often your values for consequences will be dependant on factors such as organizational policy, strategic goals, or decision makers' preferences.

Also, in Tina's situation, imagine caterer D had a better reputation than caterer C. This would force her to make a more subjective trade-off.

In this case, Tina could subjectively state the reputation of a catering company is slightly more important than its price per person. So she'd choose caterer D, even though this caterer is more expensive.

Question

Which further objective can Denver eliminate to make it easier to compare the remaining two alternatives?

The remaining alternatives are car rental companies A and B. The remaining objectives are "Cost per day," "Amount of deposit," and "Roadside assistance plan." For the first objective, company A scores a 2 and company B scores a 1. For the second objective, company A scores a 1 and company B scores a 2. For the third objective, company A scores a 3 and company B scores a 2.

Options:
1. Roadside assistance plan
2. Amount of deposit
3. Cost per day

Answer

Option 1: This option is incorrect. The amount of deposit is the objective that should be canceled, as that amount can be added to the cost. The objectives of overall cost and inclusion of a roadside assistance plan can then be compared and the appropriate company chosen.

Option 2: This is the correct option. If the objective regarding the amount of deposit is removed, its numerical value can be added to the objective of cost. Denver can then compare the objectives of overall cost and inclusion of a roadside assistance plan to make the appropriate choice of company.

Option 3: This is an incorrect option. The objective that Denver should remove in this case is the amount of deposit. This amount can be added to the objective of cost, so that in the end, the objectives of overall cost and inclusion of a roadside assistance plan can be compared and the appropriate company chosen.

Question

64. Problem-Solving and Decision-Making Strategies

Which company represents the best alternative in Denver's case?

Once the "amount of deposit" objective is removed, the remaining objectives are "Cost per day" and "Roadside assistance plan." For the first objective, company A scores a 2 and company B scores a 1. For the second objective, company A scores a 3 and company B scores a 2.

Options:
1. Company B
2. Company A

Answer

Option 1: This option is correct. Rental company B is clearly the better alternative, as its cost is lower than rental company A's cost and it offers a better roadside assistance plan.

Option 2: This option is incorrect. Rental company B is the best alternative in Denver's case, as its cost is lower than rental company A's cost and it offers a better roadside assistance plan.

Using Your Intuition in Decision Making

Intuition plays an important role in decision making, especially when decisions are complex, ambiguous, or urgent. Your experiences, memories, conditioning, pattern recognition, and inherent knowledge all contribute to your intuition, which can aid rational decision-making. Following your instincts also improves confidence, which in turn can improve your decision-making skills.

The best approach to decision making involves balancing both intuition and logic, so that they complement one another.

Intuition vs. rational decision making

Say you work in a recruitment company, and you've just finished interviewing four candidates for a position. One of the candidates is statistically better than the others. However, your gut tells you to go with a different candidate.

You can define intuition as the thoughts or feelings that guide your decisions. Other terms for this include instinct, gut feeling, or hunch.

Some people rely heavily on their intuition to make decisions. This may be because they develop the habit of trusting their intuition or because they lack the tools and processes to analyze alternatives rationally.

Others feel that instinct should have no part in decision making, and that the process should be purely rational.

A rational decision-making process includes six steps. You analyze a situation, formulate the issues, and determine the objective a decision must meet. You then evaluate alternatives logically to decide which is best, implement your decision, and, finally, monitor the implementation process and adjust it where necessary.

A strictly rational approach leaves little or no room for intuition. But this isn't always a good thing. In fact, it can be necessary – or even desirable – to rely on your intuition when making business and personal decisions.

You might not be able to put your finger on the reason why you favor one job candidate over another, for instance. But this doesn't necessarily mean there's no foundation for the instinctive preference you have.

Intuition isn't purely a random feeling or emotion. Instead it involves many factors, including your past experiences, your memories, conditioning you've learned, your innate pattern recognition, and your inherent knowledge.

Experiences

The experiences you've had help shape your perceptions and expectations. You also carry what you've learned from them into new situations. They create a reference point from which to approach new decisions.

Memories

Your memories of actions that had either positive or negative consequences in the past are likely to inform your judgment of new situations.

Conditioning

Without realizing it, people are conditioned to deal with situations in specific ways, based on how

64. Problem-Solving and Decision-Making Strategies

they've been taught or how they've dealt with similar situations in the past. If a particular type of decision or action was repeated and led reliably to a positive outcome in the past, implementing it again can become almost a matter of habit. This is sometimes a positive thing.

In an emergency, for example, it may mean that you're able to respond quickly with a workable solution, without requiring time to think.

Pattern recognition

The ability to recognize patterns plays a big part in your intuition. Consciously, or even subconsciously, your mind is able to link different areas or spot certain patterns.

Remarkably, pattern recognition is also used in rational analysis. Good managers are able to use their intuition to spot patterns linking different data. They're able to think laterally and perceive the situation from different perspectives. So, even though they are using rational decision making, they also use their natural instinct.

Inherent knowledge

You brain processes and stores information all the time. When you're making a decision, it may draw on the inherent – or tacit – knowledge you've accumulated, without you even realizing it.

Sorin Dumitrascu

In many situations, including personal and work life, trusting your instinct is a natural reaction. And more often than not, instinct is more desirable. In some situations, there is no choice but to rely on your intuition when making decisions – for example, if there's not enough time to do extra research and the decision needs to be made urgently. Or, perhaps there's just not enough factual information, or the decision is too complex and ambiguous to research every possible outcome.

Not enough time

It can be very unnerving if the situation is moving fast and constantly changing when a decision needs to be made. As a result, some people feel more at ease about going through rational processes. But what if there's no time? Rational processes alone may not help you make the most effective decision. In this case, using your intuition in decision making is necessary.

Not enough factual information

Sometimes a decision can be very ambiguous, and there's not always a lot of information to work with. A good example is decision making in a new, emerging market. There's no previous knowledge or experience of the market. In this case, you have no choice but to include intuition in your decision

64. Problem-Solving and Decision-Making Strategies making.

Decision too complex and ambiguous

Using your instinct and natural insight plays a big part in complex, ambiguous, or urgent decision making. In fact, the more complex and difficult the decision, the more important and useful it is to use your intuition. In fact, high-level business decisions are such that there isn't always time to thoroughly analyze every alternative available to you. You have to rely on your business judgment.

Generally, you can classify decisions into two types:
- soft decisions that don't have much hard data, and
- hard decisions that are based on hard data.

Intuition tends to play a larger role in soft decisions. Business areas such as marketing, communication, and people management usually benefit from intuition. However, information and data can still be useful.

In other areas, such as planning, process management, and finance, more hard data is available for analytical approaches. Nevertheless, using intuition as well as considering the hard data can help lead to a more effective decision.

Regardless of whether you're making "hard" or

"soft" decisions, intuition, knowledge, and the confidence required to make a decision are what's important.

Confidence can also improve your decision-making skills. For example, it enables you to act decisively and optimally, and can help give you a clear sense of priority. It can also help you generate creative alternatives and determine which rational, logical angles should be explored.

Question

In which types of decisions does intuition generally play a larger role?

Options:

1. Determining next quarter's budget
2. Planning and scheduling a new project
3. Deciding a marketing approach for a new product
4. Making decisions involving people management

Answer

Option 1: This option is incorrect. Deciding budgets is generally classified as a "hard" decision, and as such usually requires a lot of facts and qualitative data. However, it's also good to use your intuition if the situation arises.

Option 2: This option is incorrect. Project

64. Problem-Solving and Decision-Making Strategies planning and scheduling are considered "hard" decisions, as they require a lot of qualitative data on which to base decisions. Hard decisions tend to rely less on intuition. That said, you should always be willing to use your intuition if appropriate.

Option 3: This is a correct option. Marketing decisions are generally considered "soft" decisions. Intuition plays a bigger role in these types of decisions.

Option 4: This is a correct option. People management, usually considered a "soft" area, will often require you to use your intuition and experience.

Balancing intuition with logic

Pattern recognition is an important area in decision making. It enables you to understand situations quickly, recognize what actions to take, apply past experiences from different areas, and spot potential future problems.

Pattern recognition requires effective analysis and, while rational techniques can help, the ability to recognize patterns requires more. It requires lateral thinking and knowledge from multiple domains and past experiences. It requires intuition.

Similarly, trying to adapt a single approach to decision making will have limitations. An overly rational approach to decision making can ignore instinct and past experiences. And an over-reliance on emotions and intuition can result in flawed judgment. Both lead to ineffective decision making.

But remember, the intuitive and rational decision-making processes are not mutually exclusive.

When using intuition in your decision-making, you should combine it with other rational processes to create an effective balance between creativity and rational boundaries. As well as complementing each other, the two approaches keep each other in check. The secret to getting intuitive and rational decision

64. Problem-Solving and Decision-Making Strategies

making to work together is to evaluate the decision until you get to the point where your logical and intuitive perspectives are in harmony and balance. This empowers you to make effective and difficult decisions.

Question
Which statements about the role of intuition in decision making are valid?

Options:
1. Your intuition involves the ability to recognize patterns, which is also an advantage for rational decision making
2. Emotion and intuition are linked and used in decision making
3. Instinct is knowledge you acquire through experience
4. Using intuition alone results in the best decisions
5. It's best to use a combination of rational analysis and intuition when making decisions
6. If a situation is constantly changing, it's especially important to use strictly rational analysis

Answer
Option 1: This is a correct option. Being able to spot patterns is an aspect of intuition, as well as being useful when rationally analyzing data.

Option 2: This is a correct option. Your emotions guide your decisions. For example, if you don't think a decision will be successful, you'll feel anxious and unsure. But if you're sure about the decision, you'll feel confident.

Option 3: This option is correct. Instinct is a very useful form of tacit knowledge that is brought up subconsciously when using your intuition to make a decision.

Option 4: This is an incorrect option. Using either intuition or purely logical decision–making techniques on their own has limitations. They should be combined.

Option 5: This option is correct. Rational analysis and intuition both have limitations. Intuition lacks a grounding of reality, and rational analysis lacks creativity. So it's best to combine these.

Option 6: This is an incorrect option. In a constantly changing situation, you can't always accurately predict what's going to happen. In this case, you have to rely at least in part on intuition.

www.ingramcontent.com/pod-product-compliance
Lightning Source LLC
Chambersburg PA
CBHW031608210526
45464CB00004B/1478